# AROUND AMSTERDAM'S IJ BANKS

# AROUND AMSTERDAM'S IJ BANKS

## FROM ARCHITECTURE AND ART TO GREEN AND NEW DEVELOPMENT AREAS

**Sabine Lebesque**

**With contributions by:** Pito Dingemanse, Ronald Hooft, Maarten Kloos, Harkolien Meinsma, Ton Schaap

Valiz, Amsterdam
Noordwaarts Planning Office, Amsterdam

# CONTENTS

MÖVENPIC

AMER
KORTENHOEF

RENÉ GROTENDORST

# FOREWORD

Now that the IJ has finally become the real river of the city again, the time has come to chart an IJ route for Amsterdam residents and visitors with an overview full of interesting information about history, architecture, art and all sorts of other aspects. It offers new insights but especially new experiences of the surroundings by bike, on foot or from the water.

I have lived in North Amsterdam for around thirty years and have often been asked with barely concealed puzzlement what I found so special there. North was at any rate not a part of Amsterdam, and that idea has been emphasised for a long time – too long – by the district authority itself.
Still, in the end various developments have led to North's increasingly becoming integrated with the city. It started with the development of the South Bank: first the eastern docklands and the grain silo and Silodam to the West. And now the whole intervening tract is reaching completion, bringing the IJ literally back into sight again for the first time.
There were also a couple of important push factors on the North Bank: in the first place, the development of the former NDSM wharf as a haven for artists, craftspeople and festival celebrators. The decision to construct the North-South Line and the purchase of the Shell terrain have also had a major impact on the development of the North Bank of the IJ.
Equally decisive was the decision of the political administrators of the North district and the central city to see the IJ no longer as a barrier but as a link and to cooperate with one another. That was the basis for the establishment of the Noordwaarts Planning Office that steered the development of the North Bank for the city and the district authorities. I was director of that bureau from its foundation in 2004 until 2010, joined later by the South Bank Project Bureau.
During that period a lot was invested in the development of the North Bank, and the South Bank reached the stage of completion. Even though the crisis has slowed down the pace, the development of the banks of the IJ is now unstoppable.

The best farewell present that I could imagine was to make those banks of the IJ with their history, developments, urban design and architecture, art and areas for relaxation more accessible to a broader public. That was how the idea took shape of allowing both riverbanks to speak at the same time, to show where you can cross and make a round trip of the IJ.

I hope that you will enjoy it as much as I have been able to do for so many years.

**René Grotendorst**
*Former director Noordwaarts Planning Office*
*Chairman of the board, Rochdale housing corporation*

SABINE LEBESQUE

# THE IJ AS THE CENTRE OF THE CITY

Although Amsterdam is named after the River Amstel, on whose banks the first buildings went up, it is still the IJ that is the natural feature to which the Dutch capital owes its raison d'être. It was the city's open link with the Zuiderzee, and later the connection with the North Sea via the North Sea Canal, that enabled Amsterdam to become the small metropolis that it is today. It was shipping above all else that brought the city its Golden Age in the sixteenth and seventeenth centuries.
As in many other cities, the service industry has become the dominant sector in the past few decades. For Amsterdam, however, the relation with the water via the canals, the hinterland and especially the harbour – the fourth largest in Europe in spite of being invisible to the local population – is still of crucial importance for the functioning of the city and its future development.

The transformation of the South Bank of the IJ is already at an advanced stage, but it has only just begun on the opposite side. The local authority played a clear role in setting the direction of the development of the South Bank. Based on the idea of 'anchors' – buildings open to the public – and the breaking down of the long riverbank into sections, each with its own urban atmosphere, the development successfully got off the ground in the 1990s, profiting from the economic conjuncture of the last fifteen years.
That is how developments began on the North Bank initially, but the economic crisis and the rapid collapse of the real estate market have made it necessary to review the earlier plans. Unlike the development of the South Bank, that of its northern counterpart is expected to be elaborated with less attention to detail. Sections have been demarcated and the parameters and rules of play have been laid down by the local authority, but there is no longer a fixed final picture on the drawing board to show what it is supposed to look like in the future. What is evident, however, is that the qualities of the North Bank are such that they will form a major contribution to making the northern district that is enclosed within the A10 ring road much more a part of the city.

The role and significance of the IJ have changed dramatically over the last thirty years. A zone that was once completely orientated towards shipping and industry is now full of offices and riverside amenities dominated by culture and the media. Moreover, the water is now regarded as an environmental quality, which is why more public and recreational facilities are being implemented on the water itself as well as on its banks. This transformation is not exclusive to Amsterdam. Cities are reinventing themselves all over the world, making full use of a waterfront position and selling it off in lots. This trend can be seen in Barcelona, Bilbao, Lisbon, Baltimore, New York, Hamburg, Duisburg, Istanbul, London and Copenhagen, to name just a few.

The unusual feature of Amsterdam is that the development has been an integral one through the deliberate intertwining of public and private functions. Besides offices, large-scale housing and many public buildings have gone up on the banks of the IJ, such as the Amsterdam Public Library, the Conservatory, the music venue Muziekgebouw aan 't IJ, the De Zwijger Warehouse multimedia centre, the magistrate's court, and the EYE (the former Filmmuseum). As a result, the banks of the IJ now belong to everybody. The water is gradually assuming a new place in the world that residents, visitors and users experience. Young people borrow a DVD from the Public Library, tourists opt for a boat trip down the River IJ, followed by lunch at a restaurant by the water, and companies choose to locate their offices beside the water to strengthen their identity: it seems to be turning into the centre of the city.

The selection of projects in this guide is intended to stay as close as possible to the water. The difference between the two riverbanks immediately becomes clear. The buildings on the South Bank have in fact evolved parallel to the IJ, and the quays follow the line of the water with few exceptions. The development of the North Bank – the most attractive because it catches the sun – is still mainly at the drawing board stage. In fact it continues to be a fragmented strip. At many points it is not yet open to the public because of industry, and there are only scattered recreational facilities here and there. It is the very difference between the two riverbanks that makes it so interesting to discover them and to enjoy the surprise of constantly changing perspectives.

The more than two hundred buildings, zones, greenery and art on both banks of the IJ that are covered by this guide are just a selection of what that waterfront has to offer. No attempt has been made to be comprehensive. What we have tried to do is to include a wide range of projects that raise questions for some reason or other. Why is this building here, why it this terrain empty, what does this monument stand for, what did the artist mean his work to convey, what is the history of this house or boat, after whom is this project named, why is this building so ugly or so beautiful, who is the user, what is going to happen on this spot or in this area?

By considering all that is going on for 25 kilometres between the A10 ring road in the West via the North Bank to the A10 in the East and back along the South Bank, you can gain insight into the past, present and future of the city. The projects, each with its own story, can be seen on foot, by bike or from the water in a succession of routes. The texts by various contributors go into certain themes in more depth: the history, the light, the developments, the bridges, and the harbour in which the River IJ is still the protagonist.

HARKOLIEN MEINSMA

# THE IJ, THE VITAL ARTERY OF AMSTERDAM

## THE IJ, THE BOUNDARY WITH THE SEA

Once upon a time Amsterdam was on the coast. The River IJ was an outlet of the Zuiderzee, which was connected via the North Sea with the oceans. The spirit of enterprise and commerce of Amsterdam was decisive for its success as a port, but the advantages of the specific location beside the River IJ were a condition of that success.

For centuries the IJ was a curiously shaped mud flat that extended westwards to the dunes. Amsterdam was in the southwestern corner of the Zuiderzee at the point where it joined the IJ. This was the narrowest point of the IJ, where it could be crossed in a rowing boat to the Volewijk, a spit that extended from the old Waterlandse Zeedijk two kilometres into the IJ. This narrowing of the IJ caused strong tidal movements that guaranteed the depth of the harbour.

On the strength of these natural advantages, Amsterdam gradually assumed a key position in the trade between the Baltic and the Southern Netherlands. Particularly when shipping took on an international character and the ocean-going vessels became too large to sail on the inland waterways, Amsterdam was in the ideal position for the transfer of cargoes to smaller vessels. Products from all over the world were stored, traded and shipped in Amsterdam.

Amsterdam made sure that it was the ideal port not only for import, but also for export. When the city obtained the right to exact levies in 1650, a tollhouse was built on the Volewijk, followed by a ferry and a canal for barges, making the province of North Holland the hinterland of Amsterdam.

However, not all trade passed through the Volewijk. A number of dyke villages sprang up along the Waterlandse Zeedijk. From East to West they were Durgerdam, Schellingwoude, Nieuwendam, Buiksloot and Oostzaan. Nieuwendam, where grain was traded and a lot of shipbuilding was done, was particularly successful. Many ships returning from the Dutch East Indies favoured the protected bay of Nieuwendam to spend the winter. All the same, Nieuwendam was not allowed to become big. As a measure against competition, Amsterdam ruled that all skippers from the Amsterdam area were only allowed to trade their wares via Amsterdam.

Amsterdam expanded eastwards and westwards along the southern bank of the IJ. The actual harbour consisted of a double row of piles stretching across the waterfront. Smaller vessels were moored inside, the larger ones outside. This row of piles grew from six hundred metres to four kilometres by about 1650. In its heyday, Amsterdam was sometimes visited by more than five thousand ocean-going vessels a year.

## FROM SEA TO CANAL

Amsterdam is no longer on the coast, but the IJ is still of vital importance for Amsterdam as a port, even though the ships now set out westwards instead of eastwards.

The developments followed one another in quick succession after 1800. To guarantee the accessibility of Amsterdam to larger vessels, King Willem I decided to construct a canal from Den Helder to Amsterdam, the North Holland Canal. It was opened in 1828. To ensure sufficient depth, the sluice in the sea dyke at Buiksloot was replaced by the Willemsluis at the start of the canal for barges over the Volewijk. The rows of piles extending from the Oosterdok to the Westerdok were turned into dykes with sluices so that ships could safely moor inside at low tide. A tract of open waterfront was still preserved in between. However, this situation soon proved to be inadequate. The North Holland Canal route took up too much time and it was difficult for big ships to pass one another. In 1849 a private engineer in Amsterdam called Froger came up with the idea of opening a canal through the dunes in the narrowest part of Holland to create the shortest route to the sea. That became the North Sea Canal, a canal between two sluices. The Oranjesluizen in the dyke that closed the IJ off from the Zuiderzee were finished in 1872, followed by the sluices at IJmuiden in 1876. The IJ west of Amsterdam was drained at the same time as the construction of the canal.

## THE IJ AS INDUSTRIAL SITE

Now that the link with the sea and the hinterland was secure, the rest of the history of the IJ is one of creating artificial islands and opening up the banks again in response to rival functions. Broadly speaking, the two sluices and the canal were enlarged and widened on several occasions under the influence of changes in shipping. The surface area of the IJ near Amsterdam was gradually reduced. For instance, it was decided to construct the Central Station on the IJ, making use of the dykes of the Oosterdok and Westerdok for the rails. It was opened in 1889.

A flourishing shipbuilding and engine industry grew up on new artificial islands: the eastern islands and the land that was created by filling in the inlets on the northern bank. Most of this industry disappeared again as soon as it became cheaper to build ships elsewhere. The Amsterdam transshipment and port activities have been steadily transferred seawards. The growth in importance of road transport led to a decline in that of the IJ as an industrial site.

## THE IJ, PART OF THE CENTRE OF AMSTERDAM

Although the northern bank of the IJ always played an important functional role for Amsterdam, it did not officially become a part of the territory of Amsterdam until 1921, when the local authorities, weakened by the consequences of the 1916 flood, agreed to annexation. This gave the IJ a central position in the city. The main question since then was: What form do you give to the enlarged central area, and how do you connect North Amsterdam with the historic city, while the East-West route by water, the IJ, is displaying a renewed dynamism?
With the opening of the Passenger Terminal in 2000 and the increased river transport, it is no longer cargo that reaches Amsterdam from all over the world, but people. This global development fits in well with the emergence of art and culture on the banks of the IJ. The first steps have been taken, but more is needed to turn the IJ into an international hotspot and a pleasant and inspiring place to spend time in.

# 1. CORNELIS DOUWES TERRAIN

The period around 1920, when the shipping wharf was surrounded by fields with beetroots, onions and potatoes, is long past. The rural area west of the bustle of the NDSM was gradually incorporated in the harbour landscape during the second half of the twentieth century. For instance, the strip between the dock that was made for the construction of the Coen Tunnel and the inlet harbour – which has been filled in by now – north of the present Shipdock has become a mixed business area. The first urban development plans for the Cornelis Douwes terrain date from the 1990s. Among the functions held by Cornelis Douwes (1712–1773), who came from Terschelling, was that of director of the Amsterdam Navigation School, though his reputation rests on having created a mathematical foundation for the art of navigation.
The initial idea was to create large plots, not intensively built up but with plenty of outdoor space and storage room, intended for the heavier industry. However, it was realised that large-scale industry did not really belong on locations inside the ring. Housing was out of the question as well because of the noise contours of the western area of the docks. The search was thus for a new form of urban business terrain. The building was intensified with parking on the premises inside the front façade, which has led to a larger range of quality companies. The architecture also had to satisfy higher requirements drawn up in a visual quality plan monitored by a supervisor. The terrain has been divided up into five sections, with a gradual relaxing of the building regulations from east to west. Robust materials were recommended that relate to the former riverside sheds. Firms like Union Milieu waste disposal, the production centre of the FEBO fast food chain, the depot of the Amsterdam Historical Museum, décor builders like Fiction Factory and The Set Company, and the Hulshoff archive management company have found a location on the site.
Although building on the last remaining plots is stagnating to some extent because of the crisis, the proximity of the water, the creative activity around the NDSM wharf and the development of the whole IJ riverbank are among the factors that still contribute to the magnetic pull of this business site within the Amsterdam ring.

## 1.1 WINDMILL

**Address:** Toetsenbordweg 55
**Year:** 2005

There are few places where you can stand as close to a windmill as here. With a height of 68 metres and a capacity of 2 megawatts, this turbine produces enough energy for 1,400 households. A further seven mills are planned for North Amsterdam in 2016, sufficient to supply 8,000 households. The Our Energy collective has been set up for that purpose. It enables residents of North Amsterdam to participate in the enterprise by becoming members for a one-off fee of 50 euro.

## 1.2 UNION MILIEU BV

**Address:** Processorstraat 3
**Architect:** AG Nova Architecten
**Client:** Hecon Bouwgroep, Avenhoorn
**Year:** 2005

The Union Milieu BV building is used for sorting scrap. It is brought in lorries, weighed and distributed in orderly piles around the clock. The logistics are directed from the detached office building. The façade of the hall is composed of recycled, corroded dam wall mouldings and translucent corrugated sheets in different colours. The coloured surfaces allowed sunlight to enter in the daytime, while at night the hall is illuminated and functions like a beacon on the dockland site.

## 1.3 KERSTEN COMPANY BUILDING

**Address:** Processorstraat 28
**Architect:** LEVS
**Client:** Kersten Constructie
**Year**: 2009

The austere black box of Kersten Constructie is hidden behind a gauze wall of expanded metal that encloses the terrain. The company develops and supplies steel constructions. The architects have taken the tradition of craftsmanship of the company as the guideline for the design, making the building a showroom of the different applications of the materials with which Kersten works. If necessary, the office area and the production hall can be doubled in size in the future.

## 1.4 HULSHOFF ARCHIEFBEHEER

**Address:** Back-upstraat 25
**Architect:** ITZ-Architecten
**Client:** G. Hulshoff & Zoon bv
**Year**: 2010

The building of Hulshoff archive management stands out for the façade, which is clad with a patchwork of different kinds of standard corrugated aluminium sheets. Separated by horizontal aluminium mouldings, an architectural arrangement has been designed with which the architects allude to a bookcase. The outside thus betrays what is to be found inside: most of the interior is occupied by dossier storage. Although the Law on Archives prohibits the entry of daylight, an open façade has been made by positioning the narrow office strip with windows on the street side. An ammonia-powered thermal pump provides the energy required by the whole building.

## 1.5 FICTION FACTORY

**Address:** Back-upstraat 1
**Architect:** Linda van der Sanden Architectenbureau
**Client:** Fiction Factory
**Year**: 2009

The Fiction Factory makes décors for shops, opera performances, exhibitions, stands and interiors for a variety of clients. The new premises beside the IJ are made of wood, concrete and steel with a façade clad with aluminium panels. Inside there is a walkway on the first floor with a skylight that extends over its full length to provide the working and office areas with daylight. The saddle roofs refer to old factory buildings that are still to be seen here and there in the surroundings.

## 1.6 AMSTERDAM HISTORICAL MUSEUM COLLECTION CENTRE

**Address:** Back-upstraat 4
**Architect:** Quist Wintermans Architekten
**Client:** Amsterdams Historisch Museum
**Year**: 2010

The Amsterdam Historical Museum, which has 70,000 objects, keeps that part of the collection in this new depot that cannot be shown in the museum in the former orphanage off the Kalverstraat in the city centre. The management and conservation of the collection can be optimised in the new depot, which is why the restoration department is housed here as well. The collection centre starts with a surface area of 5,600 m2, but the design anticipates the possibility of expanding in the future.

## 1.7 KEYPOINT

**Address:** Toetsenbordweg 22-26
**Architect:** Dedato ontwerpers en architecten
**Client:** Keystone Vastgoed
**Year**: 2010

The three articulated units with a half-sunken car park are composed of clean prefab concrete panels that frame the transparent aluminium membrane façades. The three units have an appreciable roof overhang and are set back in a staggered row behind the building line. Wooden shutters have been used to give the whole a warmer appearance.
The placing of the offices and workshops on the upper floors gives users an unobstructed view of the water. Extra daylight is admitted via patios on the first floor.

## 1.8 KEERKRINGPARK

**Address:** TT Vasumweg
**Landscape architect:** 1:1 Stadslandschappen
**Client:** Stadsdeel Noord
**Year**: 2009

To restore contact between the residential districts of Tuindorp Oostzaan and the IJ – a long-cherished wish of the residents – a start has been made with landscaping this green strip down to the IJ. Its character is somewhere between that of a park and a wild riverside landscape. A path flanked by sloping lampposts and a winding wooden platform through the reeds lead the visitor to the quay with a bench overlooking the water. It affords a good view of the harbour activities in the Coenhaven and the Mercuriushaven on the other side of the river.

## 1.9 FORT CORTINA

**Address:** TT Vasumweg 148-156
**Architect:** Karelse & Den Besten, TPAHGa
**Year**: 2008

Architects sometimes look feverishly for something in the context-free industrial landscape of the Cornelis Douwes terrain to give meaning to their design. An example is Fort Cortina, a multi-company building carefully constructed using masonry with a metallic pattern. The name is a pun based on three elements: the Ford (with a d) Cortina was one of the most popular family cars in the 1960s and 1970s; the Cortina company, which imports Moleskine and other products, is one of the first tenants; and in making their design the architects dreamed of a Moroccan fort with a tower to hide behind.

## 1.10 THE SET COMPANY

**Address:** Binairstraat 7
**Architect:** Studio Steenbruggen
**Client:** The Set Company
**Year**: 2008

A strip parcellation has been chosen for this section with a number of strict urban planning and architectural limiting conditions, such as a front façade the full width of the building on the building line of the plot, and parking on the premises. This complex is eye-catching because of the glass office area set in steel frames that stands on legs diagonally above the workshop. The premises are occupied by an interior and décor builder. The employees can lunch outdoors on the roof terrace.

## 1.11 SHIPDOCK

**Address:** TT Vasumweg 131
**Year**: 1920 / 2005

The riverbank in the eastern part of the Cornelis Douwes terrain is used by Shipdock, a ship repair and conversion company. It started as the Dutch Dock Company repair wharf and merged with the Dutch Shipbuilding Company to form NDSM. Later the ADM took it over, followed by a couple of further takeovers. The company started up again in 2005 with Volharding Shipyards, Braspenning Coatings and the former management under the name Shipdock, with a second branch in Harlingen. The wharf has four sunken concrete docks on anchor piles at its disposal where work can be done out of the water. The Giant 4, a gigantic pontoon 140 metres long, was modified here in 2001 to salvage the Russian submarine that had sunk, the *Kursk*.

## 1.12 BROODJE VASUM

**Address:** TT Vasumweg 97
**Year**: 2004

Many of the companies around the TT Vasumweg have been handed down from father to son, resulting in a large family of employees who have known one another for generations. They like to meet here for a meatball, hot chicken or pastrami roll. The restaurant also does local deliveries.

# 2. NDSM WHARF

The NDSM wharf is a terrain with various buildings and installations connected with shipbuilding, most of which have lost their original function in the last twenty years. Artists, urban nomads and creative entrepreneurs have gradually taken over the buildings and their surroundings. Recently other firms, mainly related to culture and the media, have also discovered the site.

All the remains of the wharf, the eastern part of which is now even a protected national monument, were from the Dutch Dock and Shipbuilding Company (NDSM). The firm started up in 1894 as the Dutch Shipbuilding Company (NSM) on Oostenburg, the site of many wharves since the seventeenth century. However, the locks and the railway near the eastern islands formed a major obstacle to the advanced building techniques of the NSM and the wharf moved to the North Bank of the IJ. The new terrain was organised with a view to the efficiency of the shipbuilding process. The plates were cut and worked in the east. The hulls were assembled on the slipways, while the carpentry workshop and the smithy were used for the technical parts and the interior. The ship was launched from the riverbank into the water on the west side of the terrain. The NSM acquired a particular reputation for the building of luxury ocean steamships.

After the Second World War a merger with the Dutch Dock Company (NDM), a shipping repairs company situated to the West of the NSM, led to the creation of the NDSM. The resulting expansion included a machine building, a crane track, a welding shed, a foundry, and a canteen. The series of buildings formed a 2-kilometre ribbon of industrial buildings. The NDSM had developed a building method for the construction of gigantic tankers by welding two separate parts together, which made it one of the biggest and most modern shipbuilding wharves in the world.

In the 1970s, however, the oil crisis and growing competition from the Far East put the NDSM in a spot. In spite of attempts to rescue the company, it was unable to stay afloat and had to close down in 1984. What was a remote location at the time proved to be a fantastic spot for the spontaneous emergence of a free state for artists. This laid the foundation for its transformation into a cultural hot spot where media, art, music and other cultural activities have found a place. As a result of the transformation, there are now more people working on and around the wharf than during the heyday of the shipbuilding era.

The new plans of the local authority herald a second period of diversification for the terrain in the years ahead. As in the case of Buiksloterham and the Hamerstraat district, this is not a design with a fixed final picture, but a framework within which form, tempo and sequence still have free rein.

## 2.1 KRAANSPOOR

**Address:** Kraanspoor 12-58
**Architect:** J.D. Postma / OTH Ontwerpgroep Trude Hooykaas
**Client:** NDSM / ING Real Estate
**Year:** 1952 / 2007

While she was looking for a new location for her architectural practice, Trude Hooykaas was cycling over the NDSM terrain when an abandoned crane track 270 metres long, 10 metres wide and 14 metres above the concrete substructure caught her eye. This construction had once been used for the final stages of building gigantic tankers. While the local authority intended to demolish the colossal concrete structure and to place business units on the quay, the architect saw opportunities for restructuring and managed to interest IDTV as lessee and ING Real Estate as developer. She devised a light construction that floats three metres above the heavy substructure. The four lift shafts are situated in the original staircases and are the links between the old and the new. Because the cranes used to operate on the side of the platform facing the water, this side could withstand a heavier load, which is why the new construction has been made asymmetrical on top of the substructure. The awning glass panels on the outside contribute to the natural circulation of air of the double membrane. Because they can keep changing their position, the view of the building varies depending on the weather.

## 2.2 GIERENEILAND

**Address:** Kraanspoor
**Artist:** Melle Smets
**Client:** Maatschappij Noordzeekanaal
**Year:** 2009

Within the framework of the HAVENsafari project, the conceptual artist Melle Smets was commissioned by the organiser, Maatschappij Noordzeekanaal, to make a sculpture in the dockland landscape. Smets is primarily interested in the human dimension in relation to public space. He chose an abandoned mooring stage – a particularly large one that was used in the past to test ship engines – and populated it with a flock of rubber vultures. The artist wants these symbols of death to give a new meaning to this modern ruin.

## 2.3 HEMA VNU MEDIA

**Address:** NDSM-straat 10
**Architect:** Bronsvoort Blaak Architecten BNA
**Client:** Amsterdam Waterfront bv
**Year:** 2010

The HEMA opened its first shop in the Kalverstraat on 4 November 1926. It was a department store for the man in the street where products were sold for round figures: 10, 25 and 50 cents. Now boasting 500 branches, the HEMA shares its main office with VNU Media in a new building next to the IJ. This has been an enormous stimulus to the business location climate in North Amsterdam. The brick walls of the large cube look rather ponderous and forbidding on all four sides. The grand view from one end to the other of the building is visible from the water. Various walls of the atrium inside have been kept free to a height of six floors. They are variously decorated with creations by art students. The entrance on the side facing away from the water is to a HEMA concept store, with a selection of all products and a well-stocked food department – good for filling picnic hampers.

## 2.4 STUDENT CONTAINERS

*Much of the land on the North Bank of the IJ, and that goes for the NDSM too, is polluted. A clean layer of ground has therefore been placed on top of the polluted soil at some points to rule out the risk of contact. Because the central part of the wharf as a whole has cultural historical value, the polluted ground here will be covered with a closed metalled surface.*

**Address:** MS Oslofjordweg 3-619
**Client:** DUWO, Patrimonium
**Year:** 2004

380 stacked shipping containers converted into independent bed-sits in the colours red, orange, blue and white combine to form a striking whole. Students can find temporary accommodation of their own here at a reasonable price. The concept of the container housing unit has been applied at various spots in Amsterdam (Houthavens and Wenckebachweg). As a result, the huge shortage of student accommodation at the start of the century has been rapidly alleviated. Moreover, the arrival of the students has turned out to have livened up the area and to have increased safety. In spite of the original plan to move the containers after five years, they will remain in the zoning plan at least until 2015.

## 2.5 GREENPEACE SIRIUS

**Address:** NDSM-pier 3
**Year:** 1950 / 1981

After serving as a pilot boat, the *Sirius* – named after the brightest star in the sky – was acquired by Greenpeace in 1981. It became a legend after being deployed for twenty years in numerous offshore actions in Europe. Moored at the NDSM pier, the *Sirius* is no longer in protest, but functions as an educational centre for the environment, life on board and the activities of Greenpeace.

## 2.6 FINLEY THE LIGHTSHIP

**Address:** NDSM-pier 7
**Shipbuilder:** Philip & Son
**Year:** 1939

The floating lighthouse on the Irish Sea the red *Trinity House Light Vessel No. 94* has been converted into an exclusive reception and party location. The Finley organisation has redesigned the interior of the ship with a boardroom and a bar.

## 2.7 POLLUX ETEN EN DRINKEN

**Address:** NDSM-pier 6
**Werf:** Verschure en Co
**Client:** Harry Smit
**Year:** 1941 / 2003

This three-master was the training vessel of the Royal Marines Institute. It was launched from the Verschure & Co wharf in 1941. The five rooms with luxurious wooden interiors and a large deck can now accommodate groups of up to 250 persons with food and drink.

## 2.8 AMSTEL BOTEL

**Address:** NDSM-pier 3
**Year:** 2008

After having been moored for a long time beside the quay of the Oosterdokseiland, the floating hotel moved to the North Bank of the IJ in 2008. The advantage is that there is still free parking in the neighbourhood. The budget hotel has 175 cabins with all mod cons and there is a restaurant for every meal of the day.

## 2.9 DE BAANDERIJ, IJ-KANTINE

**Address:** MT Ondinaweg 15-17
**Architect:** J.D. Postma / Ontwerpers Amsterdam
**Client:** NDSM / Stadsdeel Noord
**Year:** 1958 / 2002

De Baanderij, better known as the IJ canteen, the beer hall that covers the entire ground floor, is situated on the waterfront near the ferry. The two upper floors are used as offices. When the building was still in use by NDSM, it was also an office for technical draughtsmen and a canteen plus assembly hall. In the heyday of NDSM, three shifts of 600 men each came to eat here. The building was used in the 1980s by the Unemployed Shipbuilders Association (BBS). The main activities of the unemployed were playing cards, billiards and drinking, which is when the canteen got its name De Baanderij (*baan* is Dutch for 'employment'). Because of its place in the history of shipbuilding, it is now part of the cultural historical industrial heritage. After the BBS vacated the premises, they were thoroughly renovated, but the large windows with a view of the IJ were preserved intact.

## 2.10 FOXTROT B-80

**Address:** opposite MT Ondinaweg
**Year:** 1956

This 90-metre B-80 submarine of the Zulu class was built in Riga in 1956. During the Cold War it had the NATO code name Project 611. In the early 1990s it was brought to Den Helder by three entrepreneurs who thought that they had bought a submarine of the Foxtrot class, but it turned out to be an earlier Zulu class boat. Since then the sub has had a hard time and has passed through the hands of various owners. It has never become a hip club, and according to the latest reports the current Turkish owner is thinking of having it demolished for its valuable steel.

## 2.11 PANNENKOEKENBOOT

**Address:** opposite Ms. van Riemsdijkweg

Many companies offer a round trip through the Amsterdam canals, but by contrast it is fairly difficult to book a trip on the IJ. Not on the Pancake Boat. While this Dutch delicacy is served, the boat takes you to the eastern area of the docks and back.

## 2.12 NIEUW DAKOTA / MOTIVE GALLERY

**Address:** Ms. van Riemsdijkweg 41b
**Architect:** Hugo Timmermans (Optic) with Allard Architecture
**Year:** 2010

A new temporary exhibition space has opened in the blue sheds that used to be metal workshops. Nieuw Dakota presents exhibitions and other activities connected with contemporary art, often in cooperation with third parties, including important collectors, in the shed on the left.
Motive Gallery has moved from the Jordaan district to the shed on the right, where it organises its own programme of exhibitions and activities. The sheds mirror one another and have a shared semi-transparent façade. The intention is to use the next five years as a step towards a larger contemporary art centre in the Welding Shed, similar to Dia:Beacon in New York State or Palais de Tokyo in Paris.

## 2.13 CARPENTRY WORKSHOP MTV NETWORKS

**Address:** TT Neveritaweg 6
**Architect:** G.J. Langhout / Max van Aerschot architecten with QuA Associates
**Client:** NDSM / MediaWharf
**Year:** 1909 / 1927 / 2007

The arrival of the head office of MTV Networks Benelux in the former Carpentry Workshop on the NDSM site made the new function for the location as a centre for media-related companies a fact. The concern includes not only the well-known music TV channel, but also Nickelodeon, TMF and The Box. The complex of the Carpentry Workshop and the Smithy used to stand on Oostenburg, but it was rebuilt on the North Bank of the IJ as an independent workshop in 1927. The architect of the renovation applied a continuous second membrane of glass around the existing carcass to satisfy most of the technical demands of today. The exterior with the steel frame construction filled in with brick and continuous window strips has been left largely intact. The interior tells the story of the new generation. The large wooden staircase that already starts at the entrance outside leads to a gallery where visitors can see what is going on in the edit rooms on screens. The recordings are done in a black box of 600 m2, the biggest MTV recording studio in the world. There is a red box above the entrance with a glass wall in which offices are accommodated. The other offices have been incorporated on four new floors up to the trussed girders. The floating/cantilever glass box at the end of the building is the works restaurant.

## 2.14 LASLOODS

**Address:** TT Neveritaweg 1-5
**Architect:** J.D. Postma & A.E.G. Postma
**Year:** 1952

Not just the format but also the large blue sliding doors and the small white square window frames make the NDSM Lasloods [welding shed] an impressive building. It is 22 metres high and has a surface area of 6,800 m2. The steel girder and crane track constructions in the interior are striking. Like the other wharf buildings, the welding shed was positioned on the site to enable an optimal running of the production process.
For the time being the hall is used for events, but a definitive new function is being sought for it, perhaps the new centre for contemporary art.

## 2.15 SMITHY

**Address:** TT Neveritaweg 20-36
**Architect:** G.J. Langhout / Group A
**Client:** Mediawharf (Biesterbos Planontwikkeling)
**Year:** 1909 /2011

With the new plans for the Media Wharf, the old NDSM smithy with its 7,800 m2 of floor space is being redeveloped in stages. The central shed with the pointed roof will be raised to a height of 30 metres to accommodate a hotel with a sky bar on the hotel roof. The other sheds will be converted into office space, and a theatre is planned for the large hall. One of the first tenants is the Amsterdam headquarters of the energy drink manufacturer Red Bull.

## 2.16 SHIPBUILDING SHED

**Address:** TT Neveritaweg 15
**Architect:** G.J. Langhout / Dynamo architecten
**Client:** NDSM / Stichting Kinetisch Noord
**Year:** 1920 / 2006

After the departure of the NDSM in the 1980s, urban nomads and artists gradually took over the vast Shipbuilding Shed. By the end of the 1990s they were so well organised that they were able, under the name of the Stichting Kinetisch Noord (North Kinetic Foundation), to submit a plan to the local authority for its redevelopment. This initiative expanded to become the largest cultural incubator of Amsterdam and has formed the basis for the entire development of the area.
A freestanding complex of 250 studios and workshops without fittings in three units has been erected in the interior to leave the protected monument otherwise intact. It was given the name Kunststad (Art City). There are also studios for theatre groups and décor builders, a skate park, and 6,000 m2 for theatre performances and festivals.

## 2.17 KRAAN 7

**Architect:** Erik Blits, Michel Woud
**Client:** Chiel Snijders
**Year:** 2013

The architects Erik Blits and Michiel Woud would like to use the remains of the tower crane, consisting of the bogie and the crane track, as the base for a small moving pavilion for contemporary art and audiovisual media, but also for commercial rental as a conference room or TV studio. The glass capsule looks like a diamond because of the triangular windows in steel mouldings.

## 2.18 HELLINGBANEN 2, 3 AND 4

**Architect:** G.J. Langhout / J.D. Postma
**Year:** 1920 / 1927 / 1952 / 1966

Large slipways ['hellingbanen'] from the 1920s with a tower crane between them mark the eastern part of the NDSM site. Slipways 2 and 3 were combined in the 1960s in order to complete the building of larger vessels. Since the departure of NDSM, artists and urban nomads have settled in the tapering spaces beneath these ramps. At the top of slipway 3, also called slipway Y, is the Y canteen (not to be confused with the IJ canteen) specially for NDSM employees. The monthly flea market is held during the summer on and around the slipways.

## 2.19 NOORDERLICHT

**Address:** TT Neveritaweg 33
**Year:** 2008

A semicircular hangar of corrugated sheets and Plexiglas decorated with lamps, picnic tables outside and other garden furniture in the grass with a view of the water and the city – the setting of café-restaurant Noorderlicht cannot be described as anything but idyllic. In the weekends there are regular gigs, poetry readings and theatre, which wind up later in the evening with a big campfire.

## 2.20 GEWOONBOOT

*The white filling station New Energy next to Noorderlicht is there not just to top up your tank with vegetable oil, but also to recharge your mind on the bench with a view of the IJ. This is how the duo of artists Bisscheroux & Voet have combined physical mobility with spirituality.*

**Address:** TT Neveritaweg 35
**Client:** Pauline Westendorp / De Key
**Year:** 2008

The *geWoonboot* is a completely self-sufficient home on the water. Visitors are given a guided tour to show them how you can create a sustainable and innovative workplace without influencing the external appearance or enjoyable qualities of the home and without leaving a footprint. Solar energy, a low-consumption diesel engine and a thermal pump ensure that there is enough energy on board for hot water and to supply the electrical devices. It is an initiative of Pauline Westendorp, whose company NEWNRG has made buildings like G-sus in the Hamerstraat district low on energy consumption.

## 2.21 BOOSTER PUMP STATION NORTH AMSTERDAM

**Address:** Strekkerweg 31
**Architect:** Bonnemayer Architecten
**Metaalbouw:** Holland Groep
**Year:** 2006

Because of the closing down of the sewage purification plant on Zeeburgereiland and the building of a new one in the western area of the docks, it was necessary to make the sewage in the existing pipes flow in the opposite direction. Four booster pump stations have therefore been built around Amsterdam to pass the sewage directly on to the following pump to prevent the smell of stagnant water. A design competition was organised and four firms of architects have designed the containers in which the technical plants are housed. This pump station in North Amsterdam was designed by the Bonnemayer firm of architects, who wanted to incorporate the current and power of water in the design. The inflow and outflow pipes have been raised to make them clearly visible.

UNLOCKED
1968

# 3. BUIKSLOTERHAM

Buiksloterham used to be a lake where mud dredged from the city was dumped, but the mud was washed back to the city at low tide. At this point local dignitaries gave money to the local authority to set up a job creation project to drain Buiksloterham. The drainage rights were sold to the Beukman family, who had capital and experience in this field. They also received the rights to the land and soon started to trade or to exploit it commercially. It was only later that the local authority realised how valuable the land was and repurchased it in stages.

In the twentieth century Buiksloterham was an estate for heavy industry with companies such as Hollandse Betongroep, Fokker, De Vries Lentsch wharf and the Eland-Brandt metal factory.

With the implementation of the new zoning plan in 2010, the function of the area will gradually change. The local authority has decided not to draw up an elaborate urban development plan in order to leave more scope for private initiative. There are a few rules of play in this new approach, but the local authority hopes to attract a different selection of firms and a group of adventurous residents within these rules to create a mixed urban district of businesses and homes. Now that business complexes are being created and the emphasis is no longer on (heavy) industry, there is scope for nautical, media-related and other branches.

In issuing a sustainability tender in Buiksloterham at the end of 2009, the local authority rose to the challenge to make all new building in the city climate-neutral by 2015. The jury, which included the former politician Jan Terlouw, selected the four projects that incorporated the concept of sustainability in the most innovative way in their design, while the price of the land was fixed. The selection method has attracted so much attention in professional circles that the verb 'to Buiksloterham' has been coined.

## 3.1 BRIDGE 356

**Address:** Klaprozenweg near 88
**Architect:** Aldo van Eyck
**Client:** Dienst Publieke Werken
**Year:** 1955

The long bridge with the small bridge house over Zijkanaal I, formally called Bridge 356, was designed by the architect Aldo van Eyck (1918–1999), who was employed by the Public Works Department in the 1950s, where he worked on more than 700 playgrounds in the city. The bridge and bridge house, simple but pure in form, were not implemented exactly in accordance with the original design. In Van Eyck's drawing the bridge had lanterns and a pedestal for a sculpture, but they failed to materialise.

## 3.2 DE KLAPROOS

**Address:** Klaprozenweg 60

According to the regulars of this typically Dutch café, the meatballs here are a real treat. The cosy interior contributes to the atmosphere of a living room wedged between the busy road and a site designated as a transfer point. Moreover, the waitresses and proprietors Nancy and Anita provide a warm welcome and delicious filled rolls.

*There is a floating Waternet office building in the Zijkanaal I harbour alongside the Papaverweg. This thatched building is part of the new harbour of the department that keeps the canals and other water in Amsterdam clean. The biggest ark in the Netherlands, it is an example of cradle to cradle construction with sustainable installations. It was designed by Attika Architekten, who are also responsible for the former IJburg Visitors Centre that is now situated next to Kraanspoor.*

## 3.3 PATCH 12 (TENDER BSH)

*The Ridderspoorbrug over the 100-metre wide John van Hasseltkanaal-West is a simply designed bridge with poppies by the roadside. It improves accessibility to the firms in the area. The new route takes car and lorry traffic from and to the A10 motorway to take pressure off the Distelbuurt. At the northern end of the bridge lie the plots of land that will be developed in the next few years within the framework of the BSH sustainability tender.*

**Address:** Ridderspoorweg / Papaverweg
**Architect:** Marcel Lok Architect
**Client:** Vink Bouw
**Year:** 2013

The design for this block of apartments and business units on a plot of land 30 x 80 metres is a simple volume. It consists of a 'head' building as high as the plot is wide, and a 'tail' building nine metres tall. The application of robust brickwork and concrete with no-nonsense details is a reference to dockland architecture.
The sustainable features include the wind turbines that have been integrated in the façade. Trees rise above the roof behind the tall green roof edge, an allusion by the architect to the thirteenth-century Guinigi Tower in Lucca, Italy, which also has trees on top.

## 3.4 PATCH 21 – DE KAMEEL VAN NOORD (TENDER BSH)

**Address:** Ridderspoorweg / Papaverweg
**Architect:** op ten noort blijdenstein architecten en adviseurs with Deerns raadgevende Ingenieurs
**Client:** Heddes Vastgoed
**Year:** 2012

This organically shaped futuristic pyramid recalls the form of a camel. The adaptive capacity of the building enables it to adjust to new insights and technologies in the future.
The flexible internal arrangement can be modified to suit the needs of housing, work and recreation. The building cools and cleans air just as nature does and derives energy from biomass, the sun or the ground. Its green membrane and enclosed garden absorb $CO_2$ emissions.

## 3.5 PATCH 22 (TENDER BSH)

**Address:** Ridderspoorweg / Papaverweg
**Architect:** Frantzen et al architecten
**Client:** Vereniging Lemniskade
**Year:** 2012

Patch 22 is situated on a smaller plot of land than the other buildings. The plan is a hybrid construction with a concrete and steel plinth extending over the entire plot. The six smaller storeys above have a striking timber construction. The vertical segments can be distinguished by being slightly out of alignment with one another. The design is based on a light building construction to reduce the use of materials.
Inverting the prefab wall shoes creates space to conceal all the plumbing and wiring. This makes it possible to alter the flexible programme – business units and housing – at any stage.
Heating and cooling are in the floor. If there is any need for fuel, specially developed wood granules are proposed. The staircase has been positioned to discourage use of the lift. Anyway, the lift generates energy when it descends, so that helps too.

## 3.6 PATCH 41 – KEEP IT SIMPLE (TENDER BSH)

**Address:** Ridderspoorweg / Papaverweg
**Architect:** Tekton Architekten with AMIC Installation Consultancy BV
**Client:** GTP Vastgoed BV
**Year:** 2012

'Keep it Simple, Back to Basics in Buiksloterham' is the title of the design on plot 41. The name refers to the controlled use of technology.
The designers do not want to fit expensive technological installations, but focus on decentralised plug-in heating. The façade has a high insulating factor, while screens of plants serve as awnings. The design clearly separates the bare carcass of the building from its finished state. This makes it possible to put together personal modules based on function, purpose or convenience. It also enables alternate use for work or housing.

## 3.7 VOLTEN'S KNOT

*The site opposite* Volten's Knot *has been squatted. Former industrial premises have been turned into a multifunctional spot for housing and partying. There are also areas where the squatters can realise their artistic potential. A few works of art are situated in the car park. There is a small shed, Chez René, next to the building where you can sometimes find a cup of coffee.*

**Address:** Grasweg
**Artist:** André Volten
**Client:** Stadsdeel Noord, Stichting Volten 70 jaar
**Year:** 1996

The artist André Volten (1925–2002), who lived and worked in Buiksloterham, learnt the art of metalworking on the NDSM wharf, where he worked for a couple of years as a welder in the 1950s. His works of art made a name for themselves through the use of industrial products such as iron girders. He cut fragments out of them and welded them together to form large open constructions. Many of his works were made for the public domain. His work made a signal contribution to the integration of art in the built environment.
He was invited to make a sculpture for North Amsterdam on his seventieth birthday. He devised this riverside sculpture half on the dyke and half in the water. The work does not have an official title and owes its nickname to its shape.
In Volten's words, the sculpture is 'a marker on the boundary between North Amsterdam and the rest of the world, two columns like two links that embrace one another, that is still a fraternal bond between North Amsterdam and the other side of the IJ'.

*steely stillness*
*ships hail*
*my feet*
*half in the land*
*I stand motionless.*

*Bert Schierbeek (1918–1996) wrote this poem at the invitation of Volten shortly before his death.*

## 3.8 DE GROENE DRAECK

**Address:** Grasweg 53-83
**Architect:** P. Groenhart / Architectenburo W.J. Klein
**Client:** Gerard de Vries Lentsch Jr.
**Year:** 1954 / 1995

De Groene Draeck is a complex for architects and designers. The renovated shipbuilding shed originally belonged to the former De Vries Lentsch wharf, which closed down in the 1970s. It was here that Queen Beatrix's private yacht *De Groene Draeck* [The Green Dragon], named after the warship the *Vlieghende Groene Draeck* from 1623, was built. Princess Beatrix was given the private yacht on her eighteenth birthday. The red buoy in the water near the building is a monument that refers to the yacht. During the thorough renovation of the shipbuilding shed in the 1990s, the façades were opened up to allow light to enter. Since then the end wall has a large expanse of windows surmounted by a fan-shaped balcony strip.

## 3.9 LIGHTVESSEL NO. 12

This lightship was built by Philip & Son in Dartmouth, Devon (UK) in the early 1950s. It is more than 41 metres long and has been used as a lightship at various places in the English waters. It changed hands several times before it was purchased in 1995 by the owner of the De Groene Draeck complex, which explains why it is moored here. The idea was to start a fish restaurant on board the vessel, but those plans failed to materialise.

**Scheepsbouwer:** Philip & Son
**Client:** Trinity House
**Year:** 1951

## 3.10 FACTOR IJ

A new multifunctional business complex including a catering function for the public with a terrace beside the IJ is planned on this inconspicuous site. From floor to ceiling, the so-called Head and Tail Building is constructed in glass alternating with corrugated metal sheets. The interior consists of visible concrete constructions and climatisation installations that reinforce the industrial character of the buildings. The corners of the buildings are deliberately not set at right angles to one another. This creates a space beside the inlet for a terrace that extends to the IJ. This is where the catering is planned. The building is sustainable thanks to the heat recovery systems and the heat-cold storage. Factor IJ was designed by HM Architecten. The firm is located on the site.

**Address:** Grasweg 49
**Architect:** HM Architecten
**Client:** Breevast
**Year:** 2013

## 3.11 OMYA NETHERLANDS BV

**Address:** Grasweg 47
**Architect:** Architektenbureau Wim Deen
**Year:** 2005

More than you might suspect at first sight goes on in this austere aluminium container that is illuminated at night by a blue strip of light. Behind the exterior are two mills to crush minerals, ores and other stones into powder for the production of paint, kit, cleaning and other materials. The raw materials are delivered by water; there is a large vessel moored to the quay every week. An ingenious system of transport belts takes the deliveries inside. After milling, the same system conveys the products to lorries for further transport by road.
Most of the raw materials come from mines in Norway. The firm used to be called Norwegian Talc, but has since been taken over by the multinational Omya.

*Ever since 1915 there have been houseboats moored in the Tolhuistuinkanaal as a cheap solution to the housing problems for workers. The Amsterdam local authority did not start to impose any kind of regulations until the late 1960s, and the houseboats were first included in zoning plans in 2000.*

## 3.12 KAAP NOORD

**Address:** Asterweg 17-19
**Architect:** Vasco da Silva architecten
**Client:** IN.OG Onroerend Goed
**Year:** 2005

The Kaap Noord complex accommodates very diverse enterprises, from a painting restoration studio to a shoe wholesaler, and from piano rental to an ice cream production company. Bearing the instruction to densify in mind, the architects have designed a compact building by North Amsterdam standards in purple-brown masonry with anthracite grey aluminium façades and sheeting materials. A 6-metre tall entrance provides access to the street inside, which is flanked on both sides by business units. Three tower office blocks surrounded by a car park deck rise into the air from the second floor. The car park is reached by a wide ramp. By placing the car park above the business units, this project has applied the principle of the double use of land literally.

## 3.13 CHEF'S TABLE

**Address:** Asterweg 14
**Year:** 2008

The culinary meeting place Chef's Table lies hidden amid the industry of Buiksloterham. The French-trained chef Jeffrey Verwey, who has years of experience in a variety of top restaurants, offers cookery courses and conference rooms, as well as facilities for lunch, dinner and parties. The multifunctional industrially designed space has already been discovered by the creative enterprises nearby. The menu looks plain, but stands out for the unusual, high-quality ingredients and regional products.

# 4. OVERHOEKS

Overhoeks is named after the Shell tower that overlooks the IJ here. As the Company for the Prospection and Extraction of Petroleum on Java, Shell started to build the first laboratory on the site in 1905 and went on to add several detached buildings in the southeastern part of Buiksloterham down to the 1980s. After a reorganisation, Shell has relocated to a new research building on the western end of the site. The vacated area has become available for redevelopment – a long cherished dream of the local authority.

Before the area was increasingly taken over by Shell at various stages, it had a recreational function as an extension of the use of Volewijk. In 1912 the IJ Pavilion stood here with a large riverside terrace and the Obelt swimming bath. Among other activities, an open air exhibition, the First Dutch Navigation Exhibition (ENTOS) – a sort of SAIL avant la lettre – was held here in 1913. Shell was not the large company on the site, but after years of prosperity many of them closed or moved in the 1970s and 1980s.

The plans for Overhoeks, some of which have already been implemented, give the area an entirely new function: Overhoeks as a modern, compact urban district. Apart from the Overhoeks Tower and the Big Lab, all of the Shell buildings have been demolished to make way for a residential and work district with 2,200 housing units in urban apartment blocks. The building of 130,000 m2 of offices, businesses and amenities, some of them high-rise, is also in the planning.

But the biggest change in the area is the construction of the public green riverbank and the park on the sunny side of the IJ directly opposite the Central Station, with the new film museum to crown it all.

## 4.1 SHELL TECHNOLOGY CENTRE AMSTERDAM

*There are more than thirty different sorts of elm tree in the whole Overhoeks area, making this the largest collection of elms in Europe. Three of them were moved from Old West Amsterdam, where the trees had to go in connection with the new profile of the district. Steel letters and leaves incorporated in the pavement beside the river refer to the collection.*

**Address:** Grasweg 31
**Architect:** architecten van Mourik, Arcadis Architecten
**Client:** Royal Shell
**Year:** 2009

Since 2009 Shell has abandoned some thirty laboratories, testing areas, workshops, storage depots and offices that were scattered over the terrain and brought all the activities together in a new complex. This research centre is primarily devoted to seeing how the current processes and products of the Shell Petroleum Development Company can be improved: the extraction of petroleum, the development of sustainable energy, and $CO_2$ storage. The Royal Shell Laboratory was established in Amsterdam in 1914 and now accommodates one of the twelve Shell technology centres that are scattered all over the world.
The complex comprises five dark brick wings perpendicular to the IJ and linked to one another by means of a glazed atrium-like area with elevated walkways. The massive entrance is located beside Grasweg in the easternmost wing, which differs from the others in being slightly curved.

## 4.2 OEVERPARK

**Address:** IJpromenade
**Architect:** Bureau Landlab
**Client:** Amsterdam Local Authority
**Year:** 2008

For a long time the riverbank at this location was out of bounds because of the industry there. Opening the riverbank to the public was always one of the main premises of the plans for the Overhoeks district. Part of the IJ was filled in along the existing shore for a length of a few dozen metres and a strip was kept free of buildings. The wide promenade has a total length of 500 metres. A rubble embankment ensures as smooth a transition as possible from the water to the land. A fan-shaped wedge, beneath which an underground car park is planned, forms the green boundary between the planned Strip and the Residential Quarter. The plan is to extend the public promenade further to the north if the businesses that are established close to the water allow.

## 4.3 RESIDENTIEEL KWARTIER

**Client:** Ontwikkelingscombinatie Overhoeks
**Year:** 2010–2015

The western area of the Overhoeks planning zone is reserved for housing: 2,200 apartments in various price categories, 20 per cent of them in the form of rented council housing. The first stage is under construction and consists of nine apartment blocks designed by different architects. The blocks are arranged in a campus pattern comprising autonomous volumes in a rectangular street grid grouped around larger or smaller courtyards. The height of the blocks varies from six to nine storeys. The topmost floors are set back to create space for balconies and to give the floors beneath enough daylight.

The owner-occupied apartments in De Oranje on the riverside, and the rented council apartments behind in Gelria (Baneke van der Hoeven architects) are already finished, both in sand-coloured masonry and with many balconies. De Prinsendam by the British architect Tony Fretton is also finished. The exterior of the building is clad with Altenberg travertine limestone containing fossils and other minerals, giving the façade a lively appearance. The balconies have glass balustrades and glass brick floors. West of De Oranje beside the water stands De Europa with apartments that are rented on the free market designed by the Portuguese architect Alvaro Siza. The façade has a strict composition with deep balconies and is clad with white Prinos marble from the Greek island of Thasos.

De Zeven Provincien is going up next to the Oeverpark. This volume designed by the former Chief Government Architect Jo Coenen has a horizontal articulation of lines in which glass and strips of light-coloured natural stone alternate and rounded corners. De Halve Maen by Mecanoo architects and De Statendam by Geurst & Schulze architects are in the planning stage. The crisis in the building industry has led to delays in their implementation.

## 4.4 EYE, FILM INSTITUTE NETHERLANDS

*All of the names of the Residentieel Kwartier blocks refer to vessels that once played an important part in Dutch history. For instance,* De Statendam *was a part of the Holland-America Line, and* De Halve Maen *was the ship of the Dutch East India Company on which Henry Hudson entered the bay where the Dutch were later to establish New Amsterdam.*

**Address:** IJpromenade 1
**Architect:** Delugan Meissl Associated Architects
**Client:** ING Real Estate Development, Ymere
**Year:** 2011

*A village of 306 wooden houses with local amenities once stood between the bank of the IJ and Grasweg. There was a serious housing shortage in Amsterdam in the 1920s after the First World War. Temporary villages were erected to provide short-term additional accommodation. The Obelt temporary village, officially Erica temporary village, was called after the swimming bath of that name next to it. Critics nicknamed the shabby homes 'Wibaut's orange boxes' after the Amsterdam councillor Floor Wibaut. Twelve years later the village was closed down by burning the houses, thereby killing off the vermin that had nestled in the timber.*

The Netherlands Film Institute Eye is being constructed diagonally opposite the Central Station. The new name was adopted after a merger between the Filmbank, Holland Film, the Netherlands Institute for Film Education and the better-known Filmmuseum. The latter will vacate the nineteenth-century pavilion in the Vondelpark for this contemporary, or perhaps even futuristic pavilion beside the IJ. The commission was given to the Viennese firm Delugan Meissl Associated Architects, also famous for the Porsche Museum in Stuttgart, who emerged as the winner of the design competition. The firm designed an abstract shell shape that fans out broadly. It is finished with light grey coated panels that, like cinematography, interact with the light. The designers want the project, whose unusual appearance makes it a landmark, to form a bridge between the two banks of the IJ. The long staircase alongside the building offers a new entrance to attract the people of Amsterdam to the North Bank of the IJ. EYE will comprise four screening rooms, a library, a study centre, a café-restaurant, a museum shop, and studio spaces.

## 4.5 OVERHOEKS TOWER

**Address:** Badhuisweg 3
**Architect:** Arthur Staal
**Client:** Koninklijke Shell
**Year:** 1971

The name (*overhoeks* means 'diagonal') of the high tower from which the whole area derives its present name is due to the fact that the architect, Arthur Staal, decided to set the tower block at an angle of 45 degrees to the bank of the IJ. Towering almost 80 metres into the sky, the Shell Tower and the Victorieplein skyscraper designed by Arthur's father J.F. Staal were the two tallest buildings in the city for many years. All the same, it does not look very tall; it is rather dumpy and squat on its outspread white feet. But it is crowned with an eye-catching white square that has also been rotated through 45 degrees. The blocked-out shells refer to the logo of the Shell Petroleum Corporation. The interior is both severe and warm thanks to the use of wood. This is characteristic of Arthur Staal, who always tried to steer a middle course between traditionalism and modernism.

The building has a troubled history. Shell decided to build a main office on the North Bank of the IJ for the Shell laboratory management and general services around 1965. Because of the limited size of the site, the volume had to be sought vertically. It was a bold experiment, because Amsterdam had little experience of high-rise building at the time. Pile-driving for the foundation had to go down to a depth of more than 17 metres on the second layer of sand beneath the city. The initial concrete floor of the foundations turned out to be of poor quality and had to be blown up with dynamite before building activity could be resumed. A damper was put on the celebrations to mark the opening of the building by the attacks on Shell for its activities in Africa. The building is currently being redeveloped by the Amsterdam Local Authority and ING Real Estate.

## 4.6 GROOT LABORATORIUM

**Architect:** C.A. Abspoel / Dok architecten
**Client:** Koninklijke Shell
**Year:** 1929 / 1939 / 2015

The ponderous, Neo-Classical red brick Groot Laboratorium [Big Lab] was built for Shell in the 1930s, when the petrochemical industry was booming in spite of the economic crisis. The lab soon became too small, leading to the building of more laboratories on the Shell site. The company went through a difficult time during the Second World War. The occupying forces tried to use the Big Lab to their own advantage, but with a mixture of great patience, tact and sham experiments the Shell direction managed to mislead them successfully.
The Big Lab is one of the few buildings that appear to have survived the new developments. A new function is being sought, with a hotel, catering and work functions as one of the options. Dok architecten have drawn up a preliminary design for the redevelopment with a transparent extension on the roof.

## 4.7 OVERHOEKS BRIDGE

**Architect:** Korth Thielens architecten
**Client:** Projectbureau Noordwaarts, Amsterdam Local Authority with IBA
**Year:** 2008

With its asymmetrical white lines, the bridge for cyclists and pedestrians creates a link between the Buiksloterweg ferry and the new Overhoeks development. The architects have emphasised the panoramic view over the IJ. The design consists of two cylindrical steel main girders separated by a thin concrete surface. The different levels in the girders alter the view in a simple way. Holes with large rings inside them have been cut out of the higher parts to frame the view, an indirect allusion to the nearby film museum.
To keep all interested parties properly informed about the development and the apartments, Overhoeks has its own information centre next to Overhoeks Tower.

*Five towers up to 110 metres high are planned in alignment with the Overhoeks Tower. The Big Lab will continue to stand between them. Housing, business units and urban amenities will be combined here to function as a figurehead for North Amsterdam. Urban developers have chosen high-rise to accentuate the curve of the IJ at this point.*

## 4.8 TOLHUISTUIN

*At the beginning of the twentieth century there was a swimming bath in front of the riverside park. The proprietor of the bath, Theodorus van Heemstede Obelt, considered that women should have swimming lessons as well. That was a minority view at the time. In 1887 he opened the first swimming bath for women near the Central Station. The Obelt bath moved to Galgenweg in 1914. Because of the unfortunate association of that name with a gallows (*galg *in Dutch), the street was renamed Badhuisweg after the swimming bath. With the redevelopment of Overhoeks, it has now become a quay.*

**Address:** Tolhuisweg 2
**Garden architect:** P. van der Sterr
**Architect main building:** Arthur Staal / VASD interieurarchitecten
**Client:** Projectbureau Noordwaarts, Stichting Cultuur aan het IJ
**Year:** 1859 / 1930 / 1974 / 2010

What was laid out in the nineteenth century as a café with a playground, dance floor and music tent was in the hands of Shell from 1938 until recently and therefore no longer accessible to the public. Now it has been transformed to become a meeting place for the twenty-first century, and all kinds of art and culture from all over the world are on the programme.
The pavilion with pyramid-shaped roofs was designed as a staff canteen for 1,300 employees by Arthur Staal, who was also working on the Overhoeks Tower at the time. It now accommodates catering, a theatre and concert hall, exhibition areas and a hip-hop school. There is a terrace in the sun beside the river. The Tolhuistuinpark, originally designed by the municipal engineer P. van der Sterr but of which nothing remains but the monumental trees, is surrounded by four smaller buildings: Reservaat (the former porters' homes), Staalvilla, Villa Abspoel and Poortgebouw, which have also acquired new creative residents.
The organisation is in the hands of the Culture beside the IJ foundation, which won a competition, and within which various (cultural) entrepreneurs operate jointly.

*The Schommelpaviljoen [Swing Pavilion] is planned for the enclosed public garden beside the Buiksloterweg. It is a construction of beams with swings of every sort and size for people to rock back and forth together. The idea, to be implemented in conjunction with the local residents and the Stichting Cultuur aan het IJ (Culture beside the IJ foundation), came from the designer Elmo Vermijs.*

TON SCHAAP

# THE RIVER IJ IS A PART OF AMSTERDAM

The urban planner Van Eesteren believed that the River IJ should continue to mark the edge of the city. A river like that in the city leads to bridges and other expensive inconvenience. 'Amsterdam' stands for Amstel and Dam. The city must develop westwards, where the docks were. The historic city centre was to become 'city'. Office employees travelled there from the West by tram. The dockworkers could cycle to work. New West became a grid of green and blue lines. West was followed by the Bijlmermeer housing estate in the South-East, a further elaboration of the 'lobe city'. Every resident of Amsterdam lived within reach of the centre and no more than fifteen minutes by bike from the countryside. Amsterdam was finished. Then came the overflow. Purmerend and Almere had room for the one-family homes that the people of Amsterdam needed: a house with a garden and a garage, a double one if possible. The nineteenth-century districts were to be cleaned up and sanitised: more fresh air, light, greenery and parking space, less houses. Pieces of this real Utopia can still be found in the Kinkerbuurt and the Dapperbuurt. The word 'sanitise' has never touched them since.

The people of Amsterdam woke up. City formation stranded on the Nieuwmarkt. The idea emerged in other circles that more could be done with the outdated harbour piers in the IJ once the floating castles had gone. Not everyone wants a garden or a rural dwelling. Some people like to live in the city, especially those who see opportunities that arise from the proximity of other people. Building commenced in the eastern docklands in 1985, warily at first on the edge of the Indische Buurt, followed by more assured building on the KNSM island. It was to be 'city', at least in appearance. In North Amsterdam the IJ had been reached a few years earlier. IJplein replaced an old shipping wharf by social housing. It became a neighbourhood with a suburban density and a public footpath to the IJ. The designers were guided by the interests of council housing. Private parties had no interest in building there.

'Death or dishonour' was the motto for the KNSM island. If it is too far away and if urban densities are finally allowed there, then preferably with a dash of verve – better an honourable defeat than half measures. The housing corporations and the city work with someone else's money, that helped. That was the period when the vision that still directs building on the banks of the IJ today was born. The harbour basins and the River IJ would become a part of Amsterdam. They could be incorporated in the life of the city. The larger scale of the IJ could be added to the intimate scale of the ring of canals. Besides the sheltered canal quays there were the tip of the Java island, the long quays of the IJhaven and the Ertshaven, sheltered courtyards, and houseboats. Motorized traffic was diverted as quickly as possible to and from the Ring, in tunnels where necessary. The banks of the IJ would be for pedestrians and cyclists and would be public. A city would be developed like the one south of the railway track that had blocked the relation with the IJ for a century, but on a larger scale, overlooking a broad expanse of water, and with amenities such as underground car parks and lifts. The sunny North Bank was to become a green riverside for everyone. By now the side of the Central Station facing the IJ is busier than the side facing the historic city. When the promenade along the sunny side is complete, from Schellingwoude to Zaandam, the city will embrace the IJ as never before in its history, with at most the addition of a bridge. The people of Amsterdam know the value of the everyday and understand the real significance of sustainability. That is perhaps why they are suspicious of grand gestures. That is to the benefit of the IJ. The grand gesture was already there – it only had to be made visible, converted from two dimensions to three. The urban design of the preceding decades had largely ignored the experience of the everyday. A detailed scale model (scale 1:200 for the initiated) of each of the projects to be implemented on the river banks enabled a full discussion. Where do you leave your cycle and your car, how does the front door relate to the quay, the IJ, and the city? Is there public space if you go out of the front door, with people instead of an empty space?

The secret lies in the transitions, 'from chair to city', as the architect Bakema once put it. Making the infelicities in the terrain and in the course of the process visible proved to be a powerful means of binding landscape and city together. The combination of street-access housing with an intersection of tram, train and car routes in the Rietlanden demonstrates this. The scale of the city, the scale of the IJ and the passing of time all become visible at one go. Those spots that in a utopian view of urban design were probably viewed as urban design disasters were the most beautiful to me. The transition from the Java island to the KNSM island with the view of the IJhaven and the historic city in the distance is one of them. A similar triangle of grass and clouds has been deployed on the former Shell site to articulate the desired programme, with a view of the IJ and a splendid location for a public function (EYE Film Institute) as a result. A relation between the city and the landscape has been created that also appeals to the imagination in Bath, England, one of my sources of inspiration right from the start. The cityscape is carefully composed, not in one go but piece by piece. Each new move reacts to the previous moves and to the IJ. Oosterdok and Westerdok link the historic city with the IJ in terms of scale and meaning. Take the Public Library, the Muziekgebouw, the magistrate's court, the Conservatory. The green promenade on the North Bank completes the picture. As you sit in the grass and watch the sun glistening on the water, you can see that the River IJ has become a part of Amsterdam.

MOORING POST NEAR BUIKSLOTERWEG

# 5. VOLEWIJK AND IJPLEIN

For a long time North Amsterdam was regarded as 'the other side'. The other side consisted of a sea dyke with a long peninsula called Volewijk, an abbreviation of Vogelenwijk ('Bird District'), named after the many birds, particularly crows, that fed on the corpses hanging in the gallows field. The peninsula lost its shape after the coves (*hammen*) near the villages of Buiksloot and Nieuwendam had been turned into reclaimed land in the first half of the nineteenth century. Like Buiksloterham, Nieuwendammerham eventually became a business and industrial estate too that accommodated firms such as Hollandia Kattenburg (rainwear manufacturer) and the ADM (Amsterdamse Droogdok Maatschappij) repair wharf. Now it is the site of apartments built right next to the river that form part of the biggest urban renewal project in Amsterdam ever, the IJplein, with an urban development plan by Rem Koolhaas' Office for Metropolitan Architecture.

Volewijk is traditionally a place where different transport flows meet. Ships entered the port of Amsterdam via the North Holland Canal, while commuters and visitors from Edam, Marken, Purmerend and Volendam travelled by tram and ferry to the centre of Amsterdam. The trams were in service until the middle of the twentieth century. The ferry still follows the same route between Buiksloterweg and the Central Station. The construction of the IJ Tunnel and its extension, Leeuwarderweg alongside the North Holland Canal, meant a sharpening of the boundary between East and West along this axis in the second half of the twentieth century. A rapprochement is coming into sight again with the construction of the North-South Line and the restructuring of the vegetation. For the time being Volewijk and the surrounding area will remain an assortment of different urban planning interventions that can only be understood in the light of their historical background.

## 5.1 HET PONTHUYS – CAFÉ DE PONT

*Until 1795 there was a gallows field* (galgenveld) *west of the tollhouse at the southern tip of Volewijk. As in many other cities, it was located on the edge of the built-up area. Furnished with hanging bars above a circular pit, a wheel and a stake for the executed criminals, it was a rather macabre setting. The lifeless corpses were hung in full view as a powerful deterrent for the citizens. The hanging bodies could be seen from the Galgenbrug and Galgenstraat on Prinseneiland on the opposite side of the IJ.*

**Address:** Buiksloterweg 3-5
**Architect:** Dienst Publieke Werken / Marius Göbel
**Client:** Dienst Publieke Werken
**Year:** 1928 / 2002

The Ponthuys, including café De Pont surrounded by a large terrace, stands on a lively location beside the IJ with a view of the activity of the ferry to and from the Central Station. It was commissioned by the Public Works Department as an office for the Ferry Company for the steam-driven ferryboats. The Municipal Transport Company subsequently occupied the premises for a while, though the building was empty for a long time before acquiring its present catering function. By now the building, whose style is characteristic of the period of decline of the Amsterdam School, has been given the status of a Municipal Monument.
The Ponthuys was probably designed by P.L. Marnette, who worked for the Public Works Department in the late 1920s and also designed a lot of street furniture, including the electrical distribution boxes that remained in use for a long time.

*In 1664 Rembrandt van Rijn made two sketches of the lifeless body of Elsje Christiaens, a servant girl from Denmark who had received the death penalty. To do so he rented a boat to take him to the gallows field. The novel* De schilder en het meisje *[The painter and the girl] (2010) by Margriet de Moor is about this story.*

## 5.2 TOLHUIS

**Address:** Buiksloterweg 7
**Architect:** W. Springer / Theo Bosch
**Client:** Dienst Publieke Werken / Amsterdam Local Authority
**Year:** 1859 / 1990

The possibility of crossing the water in small boats at the point where the Amstel flowed into the IJ is the main reason why Amsterdam emerged at precisely this point beside the River IJ. Volewijk is the peninsula beyond the sea dyke that penetrated into the IJ, making this the shortest crossing. In 1650 the government of the County of Holland issued Amsterdam with a permit to construct a barge canal with a tow-path over Volewijk. From then on Amsterdam was allowed to exact a toll. The first tollhouse was directly on the riverbank.
The situation changed with the construction of the North Holland Canal. The old tollhouse was demolished. The municipal architect W. Springer designed the existing building, which was opened in 1859. A livery stable was built next to it. In 1990 the architect Theo Bosch converted the tollhouse into a restaurant and wedding location and added the rounded extensions.

## 5.3 FORMER POLICE STATION

**Address:** Buiksloterweg 9b
**Architect / Client:** Dienst Publieke Werken
**Year:** 1918

This striking building in the rural style of the Amsterdam School in a bend in Buiksloterweg beside the North Holland Canal was the first police station in North Amsterdam. It accommodated the municipal police and later the water police. It is timbered on the outside and consists of two connected square buildings with tent-shaped roofs. It is now a national monument and is privately occupied.

## 5.4 NORTH HOLLAND CANAL

**Address:** Buiksloterweg / Sixhavenweg
**Client:** Willem I
**Year:** 1824

The North Holland Canal enters the IJ directly opposite the Central Station. For the construction of the canal between 1819 and 1824, more than 10,000 workers were employed to deepen, widen and connect the various canals between Amsterdam and Den Helder. The construction of this canal cost 11 million guilders (almost 5 million euro), but that was of no concern for King Willem I. He wanted to improve shipping to the port of Amsterdam to boost the flagging economy. By making use of the North Holland Canal, ships no longer had to moor off Pampus or at other shallow locations in the IJ. Moreover, the canal enabled vessels to reach Amsterdam in two days, though they needed the help of horsepower to do so, as the route was too narrow and winding for them to make it on their own. After the opening of the North Sea Canal in 1876 the importance of Den Helder as a port declined and the canal was only used for regional shipping and water management.

## 5.5 WILLEMSLUIS

**Address:** Sixhavenweg 14a
**Hydraulic engineer:** Jan Janszoon Blanken
**Year:** 1824 / 1968

The Willemsluis [Willem Sluice] was originally a marine sluice – the largest in the world when it was built. The Oranjesluizen at Schellingwoude had not yet been built at that time. The Willemsluis was designed by the hydraulic engineer and Inspector General under Willem I, Jan Janszoon Blanken. Functioning as a gateway between the IJ and the North Holland Canal, the complex has double locks. An unusual feature is that there is a big and a small chamber. A plaque on the IJ side of the sluice commemorates the renovation in 1868, which was possible because the recently constructed Willem III Sluice provided a bypass. The Willemsluis is still in use today for river boats and recreation. The operation of the main chamber is run by the province of North Holland. The small chamber is for manual operation but is awaiting renovation.

## 5.6 NORTH-SOUTH LINE TUNNEL

**Address:** Sixhaven
**Year:** 2003 / 2017

Just in front of the Willemsluis where the North Holland Canal flows into the IJ there is a mound of grass in the water: it is the top of the tunnel for the North-South Line. This metro line connecting North with South Amsterdam goes under the IJ. The plans for the North-South Line date from as long ago as 1968, but it was not until 2003 that actual construction work began. It was initially supposed that the project would be completed by 2011, but various problems soon cropped up: the collapse of several buildings as a result of leaking dam walls, delays caused by activities around the Central Station, and costs three times as high as the original budget, although the North Amsterdam part of the tunnel was finished on time and within the budget. The whole North-South Line is expected to open in 2017.

## 5.7 WVDS – SIXHAVEN

*Passing vessels are welcome in Sixhaven. There are moorings for craft with a maximal length of 15 metres. The rates vary from 10 to 30 euro a day depending on the length of the boat and include drinking water, electricity and use of shower and toilet facilities. It is not possible to reserve a mooring.*

**Address:** Sixhaven
**Year:** 1917

Sixhaven, with permanent moorings and a harbour for passing vessels, was created by digging out a strip between the sluices. The harbour owes its name to Willem Six, who was chairman of the Royal Dutch Sailing and Rowing Club (KNZRV) that used to have its quarters here. The royal cabin cruiser *Piet Hein* was moored here until a few years after the Second World War. During the construction of the IJ Tunnel the jetty was used for ship storage, but afterwards Sixhaven went into decline. The Dock and Shipbuilding Water Sports Club (WVDS), which had to leave the NDSM wharf, moved here in 1974. Its members were workers in the dock and shipbuilding industry who liked to build boats in their spare time.

*To get a better view of the IJ and the Central Station it is worthwhile to walk past Sixhaven in a southwardly direction and to take a look from where the houseboats are moored. There is a strip of unspoilt grass beside the river where you can enjoy the view of the IJ in peace and quiet.*

## 5.8 HARBOURMASTER'S HOUSE

**Address:** Sixhavenweg 27
**Architect:** H.A.J. and J. Baanders
**Year:** 1919

This delightful house in a corner of Sixhaven with an unusual roof that is curved on one side was originally built as the harbourmaster's house. The design is a combination of a rural architectural style and the Amsterdam School. It is one of the many designs by the Baanders firm of architects whose practice extended over several generations. Among the buildings they designed are the Amsterdams Lyceum (1920) in the Valeriusplein and the Blue Teahouse (1937) in the Vondelpark. Thanks to the many commissions that it received and to the cooperation with Michel de Klerk, this firm was already responsible at an early stage for the extension of the Amsterdam School style outside the capital.

## 5.9 WILLEM III-SLUIS

**Address:** Sixhavenweg 3
**Engineer:** J.F.W. Conrad
**Year:** 1866

The Willem III-sluis [Willem III Sluice] is situated next to the smaller Willemsluis, but is no longer in use. It is barely possible to recognise the remains among all the houseboats that are moored in the chamber, although the quay walls can still be seen through the trees. The Willem III-sluis dates from 1866 and was constructed to back up the older Willemsluis. The arrival of the North Holland Canal led to a considerable rise in shipping to Amsterdam. There was an outport in front of the sluice where vessels could moor as they waited for the next opening of the lock. Part of the construction was filled in during the 1960s for the construction of the IJ Tunnel. It forms a part of the patchwork of hydraulic and infrastructural works that characterise this transitional area in Volewijk.

## 5.10 IJPLEIN

**Address:** IJplein and surroundings
**Architect:** Office for Metropolitan Architecture
**Client:** Dienst Volkshuisvesting of the Amsterdam Local Authority
**Year:** 1982

More than 1,300 council homes were built on one of the most central points of the North Bank of the IJ in the 1980s. They occupy the former sites of the Amsterdam Dry Dock Company (ADM), the ICOVA waste disposal company, and the Hollandia Kattenburg clothing manufacturer. It was the first large-scale work to be implemented by the architect Rem Koolhaas from Office for Metropolitan Architecture (OMA). In scale it is the biggest plan in the history of the urban renewal of Amsterdam.

The main principle of the urban development plan was that as many of the apartments as possible should have a view of the river. That is why Koolhaas, designated coordinating architect with far-reaching powers by the recently appointed councillor Jan Schaefer, opted for open building strips in the eastern part and a grid of tower blocks and strips of long blocks. Different architects designed the blocks in detail for a variety of housing corporations; OMA itself designed the buildings on the edge beside the Meeuwenlaan and the Motorkanaal. The high-rise 15-storey tower blocks of the original design were reduced in height under the influence of the wishes of the residents. They were redesigned as urban villa apartment blocks, a typology that was uncommon in the Netherlands at the time.

The fact that the project on this eye-catching site consisted entirely of council housing is characteristic of the era when it was implemented. However, it was also connected with the conditions that the ADM works council had imposed on the local authority when the land was sold, namely that it should be used for council housing. If the apartments become vacant today, they are sold in the free sector.

## 5.11 AL PONTE

*The terminal of the North Holland Tram was on Adelaarsweg. This stop was called Gare du Nord or Tollhouse Station. There was a ferry service between the Central Station and the tram station to link the tram that went from North Amsterdam to Monnickendam, Edam and Volendam with the centre of Amsterdam. There was a combined tram and ferry ticket. The tram line was closed down in 1956 in connection with the arrival of the IJ Tunnel.*

**Address:** Meeuwenlaan 2
**Year:** 2007

Silvia Silvana from Turin had always dreamed of a waterside *chiringuito*. When she saw the new kiosk on the redesigned Pontplein and heard that there was a vacancy for a manager, she submitted a business plan and, to her surprise, was selected. She turned the kiosk into a little Italy. Home-made meatballs, cake and genuine espresso coffee imported from Trieste – it's worth missing the ferry for that!

## 5.12 HOLLANDIA KATTENBURG MONUMENT

**Address:** Hollandia Kattenburgpad
**Artist:** Cephas Stauthamer
**Year:** 1985

This triangular granite column was placed here in memory of the 367 Jewish employees of Hollandia Kattenburg who were deported to the Westerbork concentration camp. The monument stands on the site of what used to be the entrance to the factory. Only eight employees returned. The names of those who did not return are inscribed on the monument. The other three plaques on the column used to hang in the factory, but were incorporated in the monument after the factory was demolished in the 1970s. Hollandia Kattenburg was founded in 1911 by the Kattenburgs, a Jewish family who settled in North Amsterdam in 1917. They were specialised in the manufacture of waterproof raincoats. The firm had around 740 employees in 1940, a large percentage of whom were of Jewish origin. The factory was left undisturbed for a long time during the Second World War because it received many orders from the German army, but the Jewish employees and their families were arrested and deported in 1942 because there were suspicions of underground resistance and the failure to meet the quota of deportees that Berlin had imposed. One of the plaques shows a woman crying with the words 'To the departed (1942)'.

## 5.13 WILHELMINA-DOK

*In Koolhaas' master plan, the IJplein apartments should look out over the IJ as much as possible, but it was more important that the riverbank should be kept free for pedestrians. The Noordwal is not exactly a swanky boulevard, but it does afford a fantastic view of the water and the city on the other side.*

**Address:** Noordwal 1
**Architect:** f2B Architecten
**Year:** 1987 / 2000

This sunny spot beside the IJ is the location of the café-restaurant Wilhelmina-Dok ('t Dok for short) with an inviting riverside terrace. It is named after one of the dry docks of the Amsterdam Dry Dock Company (ADM) that used to be here. The old logo of the company, a frontal view of a ship in dock, in cast iron on the entrance is one of the few allusions in this area to its shipbuilding past. The pavilion was originally built on a smaller scale for a chip vendor – hence the counter on the land side – in Vogeldorp who had to make way for the renovation. The present management wanted to give the building a Tuscan look so they chose to have the outside painted orange. It was partially destroyed in April 2005 when a Rhine cruise vessel went off course. The restaurant was reopened after the damage had been repaired.

# 6. HAMERSTRAAT DISTRICT

The plans for the construction of an industrial terrain on this site in the Nieuwendammerham were hatched at the beginning of the twentieth century. After conducting research, the 'Committee for the drawing up of a plan for the expansion of the built-up area of the Amsterdam Local Authority North of the IJ' decided to construct a few inlet harbours here, including the Motorkanaal, the Hamerkanaal and the Johan van Hasseltkanaal to connect them. Small-scale harbour-related firms settled here because of the deep water, as well as companies that expanded later such as Kromhout/Stork and Draka. When they threatened to leave in the 1980s because of the problems of accessibility by road, the local authority decided to fill in the canals that had fallen into disuse and to construct new infrastructure. The remaining space was used to expand existing buildings and for the development of new plots of land. This led to a wide range of traditional industry in the area. A second wave of transformation has been taking place during the last two decades: with the arrival of enterprises including advertising agencies, firms of architects and businesses that focus on theatre, fashion and catering, the accent has shifted from a labour-extensive industrial site to a denser and more diversified urban environment.

The most recent changes in the area have had a rather ad hoc character. The local authority has now drawn up a new zoning plan with an emphasis on the development of a dynamic business area to which a housing function can be added at a later stage. As in the case of Buiksloterham, no ambitious and exciting final vision has been outlined. Instead a passive development strategy has been adopted, in which for the time being only what is needed to change the colour of the district is offered. The development of the Hamerstraat district still has a card up its sleeve, for if the plan for a bridge from the tip of Java island to North Amsterdam is ever implemented, it will land here.

## 6.1 AEOLUS WATER SPORTS CLUB

**Address:** Motorkade 15
**Year:** 1988

The Aeolus water sports club was initially situated in Johan van Hasseltkanaal-Oost, but with the restructuring of the Hamerstraat district is has relocated to the top of the shortened Motorkanaal. The club has a history that goes back more than ninety years and is named after the son of Poseidon who was appointed as guardian of the winds by Zeus. Aeolus kept the four winds imprisoned in a cave and could send them out to bring wind when he chose.
The harbour for passing vessels has more than sixty moorings.

## 6.2 KROMHOUTHAL / DE OVERKANT

**Address:** Ketelstraat 3
**Architect:** CUBE with Hendriks Schulten architecten
**Client:** Kromhout / Stork / Eigen Haard
**Year:** 1908 / 2010

Like many other big industrial players, Stork (formerly Kromhout) has left the banks of the IJ and the land and buildings have been sold to the Eigen Haard housing corporation. The six buildings on the site have a gross floor area of more than 28,000 m2. They have now been dismantled and are partly inhabited to keep squatters out. The area has been given a new name: De Overkant. In fact this is how people used to refer to the area on the other side of the IJ before it became officially called North Amsterdam. It is now being transformed into a temporary business site that will offer space for creative and handicraft enterprises until at least 2020. Afterwards it will be further developed with housing and business units. A characteristic feature is the enormous Kromhouthal with a length of 150 metres. It is used for events. This hall was originally built by Werf 't Kromhout. It is said that the hall had to move to the other side of the IJ to expand the capacity for the production of ships' engines after Daniel Goedkoop, the adventurous son of the Goedkoop family who owned the wharf at the end of the nineteenth century, managed to put his petrol engine on the map with a stunt action in 1905: he made the successful crossing of the turbulent English Channel in a boat fitted with one of his own engines.

*A bridge over the Motorkanaal is planned to create a continuous public route along the North Bank of the IJ. This will link Noordwal with the Stork site. Stork, a waterside café-restaurant, recently opened at Boorstraat 1, next to the Kromhouthal, in part of an industrial building that used to be full of machinery.*

## 6.3 FORMER REVERSING CLUTCH FACTORY

**Address:** Gedempte Hamerstraat 92-96
**Architect:** Titus Hertzberger
**Year:** 1932 / 2003

This almost framework industrial shed was a reversing clutch factory built around the gantry crane. Like the one in the premises next door, the characteristic hoisting mechanism at the front recalls the days when water flowed through the canal. When the premises were purchased at the beginning of this century, the sand had to wait until it had settled enough to be asphalted.
The industrial shed was renovated with loving care by Titus Hertzberger, making use of the original materials as much as possible. The old roll-down shutters at the front have been replaced by windows to provide the tenant – the Arons and Gelauff firm of architects – with enough daylight.

## 6.4 BREVO / HILAL GARAGE

**Address:** Gedempte Hamerkanaal 86
**Year:** 1914

This Islamic DIY garage can make good use of the original hoisting mechanism that determines the character of the street. Brevo, a manufacturer of reverse clutches for river craft, was established here beside the water of the Hamerkanaal from 1914 to 1983. The repair company used the overhanging hoisting mechanism to raise the vessels some way out of the water so that they could change the screw.

## 6.5 DRAKA

**Address:** Hamerstraat 2
**Year:** 1910

Draka, which is quoted on the stock market and has branches in dozens of countries, invents and manufactures threads and cables (*dra*ad and *ka*bel in Dutch), and has been doing so since 1910.
The company was started on this site beside the IJ under the name Hollandse Draad & Kabel Fabriek. Although there have been many takeovers and mergers, it is still on the market. Draka threatened to leave Amsterdam in the mid-1980s when the site became too small. The employees, however, did not want to leave and the local authority began to upgrade the Hamerstraat industrial site and to improve access. The products, that can be seen all over the fenced grounds, are used in airplanes, trains and cars, on ships, drilling platforms and in lifts and windmills, in houses and offices.

## 6.6 PONTHAVEN

**Address:** Aambeeldstraat 4-6
**Client:** Dienst Publieke Werken / Gemeentevervoerbedrijf
**Year:** 1930

The Ponthaven is situated in the last remaining inland harbour in the Hamerstraat district. This is where the ferries of the Amsterdam Municipal Transport Company are maintained. Historic ferries are also moored here.
The first ferry service at regular times dates from 1616, when it was driven by rowing and wind power. After paddle-boats had been introduced at the beginning of the eighteenth century, horses were used below deck to drive the paddle-wheel. Steam shipping followed, to be replaced in turn after the Second World War by diesel motorboats.
The harbour consists of a series of landing stages, a number of outbuildings with workshops and offices, and a crane that dominates the scene. The former semi-detached service homes with a large garden right next to the bank of the IJ can only be seen properly from the water.

## 6.7 M-LAB THEATRE

**Address:** Aambeeldstraat 10-E

M-Lab, a laboratory for music theatre, is inconspicuously situated on the corner near an industrial shed. This initiative, partly funded by the Joop van den Ende Foundation, targets the development of a new Dutch music theatre repertoire in cooperation with writers and composers. M-Lab presents one of its own productions eight times a year. In between it is mainly a venue for try-outs. The small scale of the theatre (capacity: 150) enables M-Lab to be innovative.

## 6.8 HOTEL DE GOUDFAZANT

**Address:** Aambeeldstraat 10 H

Hotel de Goudfazant is named after the song *Les Bourgeois* by Jacques Brel, which pokes fun at the middle class:
*Towards midnight when the notaries passed*
*Coming from the Three Pheasants Hotel*
*We showed them our ass and our good manners*
*And sang: The bourgeois are like pigs.*

De Goudfazant is not a hotel but a restaurant on a remote spot in an old industrial shed beside a broad quay right next to the IJ. The interior is industrial and minimalist, with a concrete floor, brick walls, tables with white tablecloths and red canteen chairs, and a gigantic chandelier made from a wagon wheel and empty bottles. The big sliding doors are opened if weather permits.

## 6.9 NOORDERGASFABRIEK

Address: Gedempte Hamerkanaal 17-35 / Mokerstraat 10, 20-30
**Architect:** Dick Greiner / ITN bv
**Year:** 1913 / 1995

The Noordergasfabriek (1913) was the fourth municipal coal-fired gasworks. Amsterdam was now able to meet its own energy needs and was no longer dependent on the rising prices of private companies. During the First World War, however, there was a coal shortage and the switch from gas to electricity was made. The Noordergasfabriek stopped production in 1924, though it continued to function as a distribution station until 1967. Afterwards the premises were used and modified by several municipal departments. They were sold and thoroughly renovated in 1995 by the timber company that is established there to become a multifunctional space. Although the building is not a monument, the chimney and the semicircular windows in the front and rear walls of the main hall are characteristic.

## 6.10 VOORWAARTS BUILDING

**Address:** Gedempt Hamerkanaal 10-32
**Architect:** H&E Architecten
**Client:** ID Makelaars
**Year:** 2008

The Voorwaarts Building has a no-nonsense glass façade set in a concrete frame. The name is indicated in large letters on the side wall. In architectural terms this complex for business units lives up to its name: it certainly is a step forwards compared with its neighbours the metalworking factory Voorwaarts (with a saw-tooth roof) and the brick Noordergasfabriek. It is mainly the music business that has occupied this popular business centre. It includes a music studio, a music publisher and a booking office for artistes and entertainment.

## 6.11 HET OOG OP HET IJ

*The North Amsterdam Historical Centre is located at the end of the lower part of Het oog op het IJ. The centre wants to draw more attention to the history of the district by means of activities, publications, a photographic archive, library and digital information centre.*

**Address:** Johan van Hasseltweg 2-32
**Architect:** ZZDP Architecten
**Client:** Bouwfonds, Kleinschalig Vastgoed Amsterdam (KVA) / Woonstichting De Key
**Year:** 2008

Complexes for business units in North Amsterdam are increasingly offering entrepreneurs who are new to the market and small entrepreneurs the opportunity to get on with the job. So does the complex Het oog op het IJ, where boxes with overhead doors and office spaces can be rented. The four-storey building at the end has a glazed façade overlooking the water.

## 6.12 G-SUS WHOLESALE & DESIGN

**Address:** Johan van Hasseltweg 27
**Architect:** Evelo Architecten
**Client:** G-sus Wholesale & Design
**Year:** 2003

The non-conformist G-sus clothing company started out as a skate shop in Arnhem. In the last fifteen years it has expanded to become an international clothing brand with a hundred stores in twenty-seven countries. The opal polycarbonate interior of the headquarters is entirely transparent, while on the outside the wooden shelves, behind which the warehouse is situated, function as vertical slats. The top floor of the offices is illuminated by natural light during the day. At night the interior lighting lights up the carcass of the building so that it seems to be floating.

## 6.13 JOHAN VAN HASSELTWEG

**Client:** Amsterdam Local Authority
**Year:** 1985

This linear street used to be a canal exactly 100 metres wide. The idea came from Johan van Hasselt, director of the Royal Dutch Steamship Company. Work started on the construction of a shorter direct route for shipping between the eastern area of the docks and the North Sea Canal in 1908. That would save the ships from having to make a bend in the IJ and, more important still, they would no longer get in the way of the ferries, which were rather slow at the time. Full of enthusiasm, work on digging out the canal started at both the eastern and the western end. It was not known at that moment how the link between the two sides was to be made – a solution had to be found for the difference in water level between the IJ and the canal and for the point where it was to join the North Holland Canal – nor who would pay the bill. Soon afterwards it all turned out to be less urgent than supposed, and although it still remained on the agenda for some time, the link was never completed. The half-implemented plan was definitively scrapped when the IJ Tunnel intersected it.
Industrial activity flourished around the Johan van Hasseltkanaal as it did around the Hamerkanaal and the Motorkanaal, until the advantages of transport by road outstripped those of water transport. That is why the canals were filled in during the 1980s.

## 6.14 NOORDWAARTS 5

**Address:** Zamenhofstraat 150
**Year:** 1992

The former Verschure wharf site in Zamenhofstraat now accommodates hundreds of handicraft firms, artists and other creative entrepreneurs. Ton Neus is unofficial 'mayor' of the complex. He started the renovations to create business units in the early 1990s. He laid floors in the main industrial shed first, and did not start on the next floor until the previous one had been rented. Through a system of varying rents, he has managed to attract a wide range of tenants in the different buildings.
One of the many artists who work here is Sigrid van Essel, for whom the urban developments on the banks of the IJ form a source of inspiration. The shifting perspective, depending on whether you are on the North Bank, South Bank or the IJ itself, constantly yields new viewing angles that she incorporates in her paintings.

## 6.15 VOGELDORP

*This was once a bath house for the temporary homes of Vogeldorp. After renovation by the Stadsherstel company, Museum De Noord is now established here with exhibitions, courses and cycling routes centred on the theme of North Amsterdam.*

**Address:** Zamenhofstraat, Vogelkade
**Renovation architect:** Marloes van Haaren
**Client:** Gemeentelijke Woningdienst / De Key
**Year:** 1919 /1997

The homes in Vogelwijk were mainly intended for employees of the big companies in North Amsterdam such as Draka, Kromhout, Verschure and the Amsterdam Dry Dock Company (ADM). The first homes were built beside the Meeuwenlaan, but the real building fever started after the First World War when the district spread out around the industries. The workers' houses in Vogeldorp were intended as temporary housing. In line with the garden city concept, the homes for employees and their families admitted plenty of daylight and were spaciously laid out amid a lot of greenery. However, after the 1980s the temporary character of Vogeldorp became a permanent one after the homes had been renovated and the garden village acquired the status of a municipal monument.

# 7. NIEUWENDAM

Until the end of the nineteenth century, the village of Nieuwendam was situated beside the River IJ. The houses and industry were thus located near the ferry mooring stage and the old wharfs of Bernhard, De Vries Lentsch and other companies. The shipbuilding boom is reflected in the many villas on the Nieuwendammerdijk. A grain warehouse and the large group of self-employed craftsmen also contributed to the prosperity of Nieuwendam. When mud from Amsterdam was dumped in front of the village in the course of the nineteenth century, it found itself behind two broad plots of reclaimed land. Only the harbour basin was left as it was to maintain the link with the River IJ. Immediately opposite the harbour was the poldered Nieuwendammerham, which belonged to the Amsterdam local authority. The Ketjen sulphuric acid plant was located here. The construction of the Nieuwendammerham did no harm to the village. In fact it meant the arrival of more employees, for whom a busy building programme had to be implemented.

By 1913 the boundary between Nieuwendam and the neighbouring local authority of Buiksloot had been reached, and the Meerpad was also completely built up. The building boom, however, was not enough: N.A. Bernhard made loud complaints that he would expand his shipping wharf further if he could only find housing for more employees. The growth came to an end in 1916 when the dykes gave way at dozens of points when they were hit by a tidal flood. The local authorities in Waterland had a difficult time too and grew impoverished. This was one of the reasons for the Amsterdam local authority to annex Nieuwendam at its own request together with Buiksloot and Ransdorp on 1 January 1921. As part of the North Amsterdam district, Nieuwendam and the surrounding Nieuwendammerham have become a transitional zone: a patchwork quilt of greenery and industry with a historic ribbon development beside the dyke, which has by now earned itself the name of the Gold Coast of North Amsterdam. With the gradual decline in the growth of the shipbuilding sector, the wharves were turned into small jetties and the buffer of greenery was redesignated as recreational land. Ketjen changed hands several times. The US Albemarle Corporation took it over in 2004.

In spite of the plans contained in the Amsterdam General Extension Plan to build a road right through the area to link Nieuwendammerham with Schellingwoude and Volewijk, that link was never implemented. It is still an area that you can only cycle around via the old dyke with its picturesque dyke houses.

## 7.1 W.H. VLIEGENBOS

*Cast iron arches eight metres tall from an old market complex in Paris mark the entrance to the Vliegenbos. They were presented to North Amsterdam by the artist Peter Diem.*

**Client:** Amsterdam Local Authority
**Year:** 1918

'Woodland for the workers, under the smoke of Amsterdam, a tract of countryside that the city needs so badly' was the slogan that echoed when the IJbosch was planted. It was named after the Social Democrat councillor Willem Hubert Vliegen after his death. Vliegen initiated the planting of this wood in North Amsterdam to attract people to move to the other side of the IJ. During the Second World War, however, a large part of the wood was used for fuel. After the war the trees were given free rein again. The Vliegenbos is characterised by ash, maple and a large variety of elm trees. It has the largest number of different varieties of elm tree in the Netherlands, and possibly in the whole of Western Europe.
Today the Vliegenbos forms part of the main green structure of the central city and has many recreational facilities, such as a camp site, a scouting group, and a tennis club.
The Buitenzorg complex of allotments, where the writer and poet Simon Vinkenoog used to spend his summers, is situated on the edge of the park.

## 7.2 ALBEMARLE

*The white wisps of smoke from Albemarle are produced by the down draught dryer. Small particles are put inside the mill to dry. The wet particles fall into a hot air current. This produces steam, which is what you see.*

**Address:** Nieuwendammerkade 1-3
**Architect:** Ben Merkelbach, Piet Elling, Jan Verster
**Client:** Gerard Tileman Ketjen / Akzo
**Year:** 1900 / 1948–1955

The white cylinders, wisps of smoke and the big fence around the Albemarle Corporation factory suggest that something very dangerous goes on there. The fact that the company specialises in chemicals and catalysts does nothing to lessen that fear. All the same, the plant does not produce any emissions that can endanger health today. Still, there were other owners before the name of Albemarle became connected with this area. The first was the Ketjen family. Ketjen had a sulphuric acid factory on the other side of Amsterdam on the Overtoom, but had to relocate because it could no longer be allowed in the expanding city. Ketjen ended up, via a detour, in North Amsterdam. Besides producing sulphuric acid, it also produced unrefined brown sugar, salt and other items. With the closing down of the production of sulphuric acid and after several mergers with the salt and other industries, its changed its name to Akzo, later Akzo Nobel. Production was concentrated on chemicals and catalysts. The factory was bought by the US Albemarle Corporation in 2004, to which it owes its present name.
Several buildings on the site were designed by the former city architect Ben Merkelbach and Piet Elling between 1948 and 1955, including the laboratory, the porter's lodge, the canteen and the bulk storage depot with the saw-tooth overhead lighting. The catalyst factory was designed in 1956 by Jan Verster, who took over Merkelbach's commissions after his death. Since their priority is the running of the plant, the directors of Albemarle are reluctant to determine the architectural value of the buildings.

## 7.3 HET FORT WHARF

*A former shipbuilding shed on the Nieuwendammerkade from the late 1930s was converted into seventeen residential apartments with studio in 2001. The buyers had a say in the arrangement of the interior. This was one of the first initiatives to make the combination of functions official in North Amsterdam.*

**Address:** Nieuwendammerkade 34
**Client:** Gerardus de Vries Lentsch
**Year:** 1875

Het Fort wharf of Gerardus de Vries Lentsch is situated at the end of the Pereboomsloot between the Vliegenbos and the Nieuwendammerdijk. De Vries Lentsch, a ship's carpenter, worked on the Meursing wharf – Meursing was a well-known figure in shipbuilding in Amsterdam. But Gerardus liked to work on the side by building flatboats in his shed beside the Grote Die. Meursing was not appreciative and gave Gerardus the simple choice of working for him or not. Gerardus rose to the challenge and started up his own wharf, which made a name for itself beyond the borders of Holland. He rented Fortland beside the Grote Die from the council and built every water sports craft of the time, from wherry to jolly boat, sloop and yacht. The De Vries Lentsch office was in De Halve Maen, which still stands as number 204 on the Nieuwendammerdijk. However, the firm was affected by many problems at the executive level: two sons set up their own wharf in competition with that of their father. This eventually led to the closing down of the company in 1975.

## 7.4 CAFÉ 'T SLUISJE

**Address:** Nieuwendammerdijk 297

Café 't Sluisje is named after the small sluice dating from 1565 beside it. The sluice was used by farmers from Waterland to bring their milk to the city or to transfer cargo to different types of vessel. This key position led to the emergence of the village of Nieuwendam, which was the link with the hinterland for centuries.

It is still possible to pass through the sluice today, but it is up to the user to operate the sluice himself. If that is too much trouble, Café 't Sluisje has an inviting terrace beside the water where you can moor a small boat if you like.

## 7.5 TWELLEGEA (MARINA AND SAIL CAFÉ)

**Address:** Nieuwendammerdijk 284
**Client:** Henk Huisman
**Year:** 1981

As the name suggests, the marine yachting club to which the marina owes its name comes from Friesland. It was very active in the 1970s and took part in various marine yachting events. The club moved to Amsterdam in 1981 because its founder, Henk Huisman, was looking for a location connected with the sea. His eye fell on Nieuwendam.

Passers-by are welcome as well as members of the club. Moreover, Sail Café Twellegea – hidden behind dozens of boats in dry storage – is an excellent spot to have a drink and look at art. The artist Ton Kalle exhibits massive stone sculptures here that he makes in his studio on the Gembo terrain.

## 7.6 ZIJKANAAL K

*There are ten side canals along the North Sea Canal and the North Bank of the IJ. They are labelled alphabetically from A to K. They were created for water management in North Holland and to link the rivers and canals with the open water. The first in the series, Zijkanaal A, runs from Beverwijk to the North Sea Canal. It was originally intended to flood the Amsterdam Defence Line if necessary.*

Zijkanaal K is situated between Albemarle and the Gembo Oranjewerf. The canal, which was originally straight, owes its bend to the former owner of the Albemarle site, Ketjen. The course of the canal was altered in 1957 to double the size of Ketjen's industrial site.
There are several houseboats beside the Vliegenbos, some of them architect-built. Nieuwendam with its big harbour is situated at the end of the canal. The small houses on the Scheepmakerskade are noteworthy. They were originally shipbuilders' houses, but they were rebuilt in the 1970s in the style of the time.
There is a smaller harbour at the end of the Pereboomsloot. Both harbours were originally wharves, but are now used as winter storage facilities for yachts. You can pass through the sluice beside Café 't Sluisje to reach the waters of Kleine Die and Grote Die.

## 7.7 RIETLAND

**Address:** Nieuwendammerdijk
**Architect:** Bureau B+B

A green zone has been left without any buildings between Nieuwendam and the waterfront activity as a buffer between the industry and the surrounding residential areas. In the past the Ketjen sulphuric acid plant was a major environmental hazard. Tall trees were supposed to block any poisonous clouds. The landscape design of Rietland by Bureau B+B has been carried out at the request of and in consultation with the local community. The cottages on the Nieuwendammerdijk have a good view of the green Rietland which now affords ample opportunity for walking and playing.

## 7.8 BOOGBRUG

**Address:** Monnikendammerweg
**Engineer:** D. Slebos
**Year:** 1957

In front of the Oranjewerf is an arched bridge over the greenery that seems to go from nowhere to nowhere. The Amsterdam General Extension Plan (AUP) of 1935 explains what it is doing there. The idea was to extend the Zuiderzeeweg to the Meeuwenlaan. This would then function as the new main route through the area. The Ketjen sulphuric acid plant was in favour of the plan because the route would pass beside the factory site, thereby optimising its accessibility by road. The bridge was constructed in the 1950s as part of the route when the AUP was also implemented in the rest of the city. The road, however, failed to materialise because of pressure from the Nieuwendam shipping wharves, which had secured the right to a free passage to the IJ at all times without a bridge over Zijkanaal K. The idea cropped up again in the Structural Vision of 1958, but it seems to have died a quiet death in the course of time. The bridge remains as a relic of a bygone era. The Structural Vision of 2010 does raise the possibility of the route again, but no specific plans have as yet been made.

## 7.9 ORANJEWERF AND GEMBO TERRAIN

*West of the Gembo terrain is one of the few spots beside the IJ where you can officially put a boat into the water with a trailer. The other one is on the TT Vasumweg near the NDSM terrain.*

**Address:** Nieuwendammerdijk 538
**Year:** 1949

The activities on the Oranjewerf are clearly visible from the water, but are hidden from sight on land by trees and fences. The Oranjewerf is one of the larger wharves in the Netherlands. It was established in 1949 as an independent ship repair company. It was taken over by the Verschure machine manufacturer and started up again under its own name in 1980. The wharf has a 100-metre slipway and a floating dry dock. The main activities are maintenance, repair and conversion. Only authorised persons are admitted to the wharf.
The Gembo terrain, named after the Gembo paint and soluble glass manufacturing company that used to be here and was later taken over by Ketjen/Akzo Nobel, is open to the public because it is now a mixed business complex. For instance, the sculptor who exhibits at the Twellegea Marina works here, there is an ironware company, and a bunker station for Rhine shipping on the waterfront. With a bit of manoeuvring you can get a good view of the Java island and the Oranjesluizen from the quay.

*When Zijkanaal K was moved in 1957, railway lines were laid down to the water at the same time so that the freight train could ride onto the rail ferry. The rail ferry had been used before, but not on this location. The rail ferry went from the North Bank of the IJ to the Rietlanden yard on the other side of the river, from where the freight trains could join the national railway network. The rise of road transport led to the closure of the rail ferry in the 1970s.*

# 8. SCHELLINGWOUDE

This sparsely populated village was an autonomous municipality until 1857, when its 140 residents merged with the Ransdorp municipality, which in turn became a part of the Amsterdam local authority in 1921. Schellingwoude is supposed to owe its name to the wood (*woud*) that formed the barrier (*schelling*) between Waterland and the Zuyderzee. The wood was probably destroyed during the St Elizabeth's Day flood of 1421. The village cottages, some of which are timber constructions, are almost all situated on the dyke beside the IJ or in the parallel street below. The village community consisting mainly of farmers and a few fishermen had already had a village church on a mound behind the dyke for a long time. The real prosperity of Schellingwoude came after the construction of the Oranjesluizen. Houses outside the dyke were built for the lock personnel. As civil servants, the lock operators were in permanent employment for a permanent wage. The many vessels that passed through the lock or had to wait for the right wind were a good source of revenue for the shops and bars in the village. The opening of a ferry service between the Oranjesluizen and Amsterdam at the end of the nineteenth century brought in even more visitors. Spending sunny Sundays in this green idyll on the North Bank of the IJ was especially popular among the city folk. The village gradually expanded as commuters from Amsterdam and the élite from North Amsterdam welcomed the opportunity to settle there. The main changes that determined the atmosphere of this village just inside the Amsterdam boundary were the infrastructural works of the bridge to Schellingwoude in 1957 and the Zeeburgertunnel in 1990. With the arrival of IJburg and the development of Zeeburgereiland, the historic village centre that was once far away from the big city has now come to lie in the middle of the urban area.

## 8.1 SCHELLINGWOUDERPARK

**Address:** Schellingwouderdijk
**Client:** Stadsdeel Amsterdam-Noord
**Year:** 2010

The Schellingwouderpark is part of the 'Van IJ to Gouw' nature project. This project is intended to strengthen the ecological link between the IJmeer and Waterland. It includes the construction of a wall for kingfishers and places for the grass snake, root vole and dragonfly to hibernate. A wide green hedge as a shelter for animals still needs time to grow.
The park also has a recreational value. The construction of a footpath has made this area on the North Bank of the IJ accessible to the public. There are small ferries that pedestrians can operate by hand to cross the channels in the park. At the opening of the park, the North Amsterdam District councillor Harm-Jan van Schaik proudly called the footpath an 'ecological route for sauntering'.

## 8.2 AUXILIARY POST OFFICE

**Address:** Noorder IJdijk 63-65
**Architect:** Cornelis H. Peters
**Year:** 1909

To the north of the Oranjesluizen stands a tall perky building. What the exterior of this small building does not betray is that it used to be a post office for inland watercraft. Given the lack of a permanent address, the bargees could collect their post here while they waited in the lock. The architect was Cornelis H. Peters, a student of P.J.H. Cuypers who also used Neo-styles in his designs. Peters had an extensive portfolio of commissions and was also Chief Government Architect for a brief period. During the last two decades of the nineteenth century his firm designed more than forty post offices, including the former Amsterdam head post office (now the Magna Plaza shopping centre). An unusual feature of this lockside building are the staggered windows on the east side.

## 8.3 ORANJESLUIZEN

**Address:** between Noorder and Zuider IJdijk
**Architect:** J. Dirks, J. Hawkshaw, A.W. Olivier, Johannis de Rijke
**Client:** Amsterdamsche Kanaal-Maatschappij
**Year:** 1872 / 1997 / 2000

The Oranjesluizen are part of the North Sea Canal complex and form the boundary between the Binnen-IJ and the Buiten-IJ. The construction of the locks was intended to stop the silting up of the Amsterdam harbour and to contribute to maintaining the water level in the North Sea Canal. Since the completion of the Afsluitdijk in 1932, they also prevent too much brackish water from the North Sea Canal from entering the IJsselmeer. The locks are also important for flushing the canals and to maintain a constant water level in the city. The complex construction – the creation of the cofferdam ran into many problems – was implemented under the responsibility of the hydraulic engineer Johannis de Rijke. After De Rijke had pulled this feat off successfully, he was invited to go to work in Japan, where his portfolio included dams for Osaka harbour and a tunnel canal from Lake Biwa to Kyoto. The three smaller locks that were a part of the initial construction have flap doors and are now used for the smaller barges and recreational boats. The Prince Willem-Alexander Lock was added in 1995 for larger inland watercraft. It has sliding doors that glide over a very thin film of water (a hydrofoot). A monument placed between the locks commemorates the renovations of 1997 and 2000.
It is possible to zigzag over the locks on foot or bicycle, but you should not be in a hurry because if the lock is open, it can take quite a while before you are on the other side.

## 8.4 SCHELLINGWOUDERKERK

**Address:** Wijkergouw 6
**Client:** Ministry of Water Management / Stadsherstel
**Year:** 1866 / 2000

Excavations have shown that there was already a church on the mound at the foot of the Schellingwouderdijk in the fourteenth century. The striking small church that can be seen today dates from 1866. It was built with financial support from the government and under the supervision of engineers from the Ministry of Water Management. Cattle were stalled there in 1916 during serious flooding all over Waterland. The original Dutch Reformed church was restored by the Stadsherstel company in 2000. This is the smallest of all the churches owned by Stadsherstel. In the interior the vault is timbered and the walls are in white plaster. The two copper chandeliers add to the romantic atmosphere, making it a popular location for weddings. The wedding cake can be cut in the pavilion outside.

## 8.5 HOUSEBOATS BUITEN-IJ

**Address:** opposite Schellingwouderdijk

Several kinds of recreational and commercial vessels are moored side by side in the inland harbour of Schellingwoude, the so-called Buiten-IJ. Within the framework of the Buiten-IJ Houseboats project, various measures are being taken to ensure the permanence of both functions and to prevent cluttering. This transitional area between the fringe of the city (the cottages of Schellingwoude) and the untouched natural surroundings of Waterland is a permanent mooring place for many houseboat owners, but there is also space for through traffic. Most of the craft moored here are no longer than 18 metres, but there are a couple of moorings for commercial vessels of up to 110 metres.

## 8.6 SCHELLINGWOUDERBRUG

**Address:** Zuiderzeeweg
**Client:** Dienst Publieke Werken
**Year:** 1957

In spite of all the plans that have been made since the nineteenth century, so far only one bridge has been built over the IJ: the Schellingwouderbrug over the Buiten-IJ. Millions of pedestrians and cyclists, people who lived or worked in North Amsterdam, crossed the river every year in the 1920s – far more than had been envisaged when the construction of the industrial sites was originally planned. However, serious plans for a bridge over the IJ were obstructed by fear that it would impede shipping. In the 1930s the focus shifted to a tunnel near the Hempont in the west. Report after report was written and the proposal for a tunnel for pedestrians and cyclists was also given serious consideration. The Public Works department set up a special Tunnel Bureau that carried out a thorough investigation of the various ways of linking the two banks of the river during the war. In the end it was decided to build the IJ Tunnel. Because of the growth of traffic in the 1950s, however, the design for the Schellingwouderbrug that already existed on paper was implemented soon afterwards. The bridge was built within a period of two years with government funding.

## 8.7 LANDJE POLS / MARCHAIL!CYCLE YOU

**Address:** Schellingwouderdijk 339
**Year:** 2009

The Bert Pols Garden Centre, which serviced the various allotments in the surroundings, was established for a long time on the Schellingwouderdijk. The premises have fallen into disrepair by now. There are plans to start a covered biological market there. At the moment there is a special cycling facility on the spot that targets sportive cyclists on their way to Waterland. You can store your racing bike and have it serviced here, change into biking gear, cycle off and eventually come back again after a training round for a cup of coffee. It is also the starting point of the annual workshop route through North Amsterdam.

## 8.8 ZEEBURGERTUNNEL

**Address:** Ringweg-Noord
**Architect:** Enrico Hartsuyker
**Client:** Rijkswaterstaat
**Year:** 1990

The Zeeburgertunnel connects the north and the east of the city beneath the River IJ. This tunnel for motorized vehicles has a total length of 946 metres, 336 of which form a sunken tunnel consisting of three 110-metre strips. With the slogan 'The tunnel is opened and the ring is closed', the opening of the tunnel in 1990 also marked the completion of the A10 ring road around Amsterdam. The entrances and operating cabin were designed by Enrico Hartsuyker, who had also designed the IJ Tunnel more than twenty years earlier. Hartsuyker, who was born in Genoa, where his father worked as a shipbuilder in the Italian port, wanted the carefully designed curved entrances to suggest that you are driving onto the back of a ferry.

RISICO

RISICO

RONALD HOOFT

# NOT ONE BRIDGE BUT TWO

There are people who find the ferries that link the quay behind the Central Station with the North Bank of the IJ rather romantic. You can recognize from a distance: identical rainwear and a his & her bicycle. Twice a year when the weather is perfect they cycle to Schellingwoude, or perhaps to the Stompe Toren of Ransdorp. There is no denying it, it is a delightful trip if you like it: past the lightning development of Overhoeks, along the canal, through the new Noorderpark – brilliantly designed by the landscape architects of West 8 –, before crossing to the village idyll of the Nieuwendammerdijk for a watery cup of coffee at the local pub. Then on past the neatly painted wooden dyke houses, the picturesque jetty and the beautiful Rietlanden – if you are lucky you can see the retired socialist leader Wouter Bos sitting on a bench in the sun reading the Saturday supplements – and then standing on the pedals for the deceptively easy climb of the two bridges towards Zeeburg and East Amsterdam.

Everyday reality is a lot less glamorous. Probably because the ferry service, for reasons unknown to me, is the only free public transport in this city – a fact that no doubt (justifiably) annoys residents in other peripheral districts such as the Bijlmer and Osdorp – many people regard the ferry as a public highway. That is undoubtedly why many consider it their basic right to smoke on board (nicotine, cannabis, or a mixture of the two), to make a lot of noise (with their scooters), and now and then to spit vigorously on the deck, or most likely, a combination of all three activities. The majority of people who stand waiting at the waterside – on both sides, by the way – also clearly find it absolutely self-evident that they do not need to wait a second to board once the ferry has moored and the ramp has touched the quay. Personally, I know of no other place where people treat the hospitality so generously offered them in such a loutish fashion.

Of course, this phenomenon is by no means confined to the ferries over the IJ, nor is this a decisive argument to abolish them and to replace them with tunnels or several bridges. Obviously there are clear ecological advantages, and imagine the enormous amount to be saved in personnel, maintenance and fuel costs. It must be simple to calculate what the abolition of the ferry services would mean in terms of $CO_2$ emissions. It is also easy to add the invoice of the diesel supplier and the wage slips of the captains and their steersmen – who spend most of their time below deck combing the *Metro* and the *Spits* and sipping cups of Senseo – to the expenditure on interest, depreciation, maintenance, repair and safety precautions.

So the dull and worn-out argument of the open harbour can be swept from the table: Amsterdam stopped having commercial activities on the eastern side of the city long ago. The merits of the cruisers that moor there have also been overtaken by events. There is now serious talk about the need for a new passenger terminal for cruisers in the Houthaven, which puts an end to that problem. The old terminal will remain suitable for boats returning from a trip on the Rhine, the organisation of a tawdry dance event, or the launching of a political movement, while the new one will be on such a scale that it can easily provide the required capacity, besides offering opportunities for a really good design instead of a building that looks like a wave (for ships! Need I say more…) This leaves everything clear for the solution that I have been advocating for some time: two bridges. The first is a bridge for cyclists, high enough for freight vessels from the Ruhr and the aforementioned pleasure boats to pass underneath, from the tip of the Java island to the Hamerstraat or the Motorkade as an extension of the Jan Schaeferbrug. It ends immediately in the eastern area of North Amsterdam that is buzzing with activity at the moment: Pand Noord (a complex for entrepreneurs in the film industry), the M-Lab for experimental theatre, the extremely hip restaurant De Goudfazant, as well as clothing and fashion companies. The bridge also connects (via the Vliegenbos) with the popular tourist route described earlier. The other bridge runs from the Tasmanstraat in the Houthavens to the Grasweg and follows exactly the same route as the ferry. This should be a striking visual gateway to the city. I am convinced that a twenty-first-century version of a combination of the Ponte Vecchio in Florence and Brooklyn Bridge is one of the possibilities. If you project this variant onto the urban development plan of Amsterdam, you see how elegantly this solution completes the ring formed by the Nassaukade, Stadhouderskade and Mauritskade.

There is no denying the beauty of the open surface of the water between the Central Station and the new film museum. It does not take a great deal of imagination to picture a cable car for tourists above it – neatly designed eggs dangling from a steel wire, high above all the shipping and with a panorama of the whole city, a dynamic and spectacular attraction that would easily pay for itself.

In the mean time there would be no need to get rid of those ferries. On the contrary, they could function as real public transport, a shuttle service zigzagging between the two sides of the IJ that starts at the easternmost point of IJburg, stopping at Durgerdam, Zeeburg, Schellingwoude, the KNSM island, Akzo, the Java island, the Muziekgebouw, IJplein, Buiksloterweg, the Central Station, Stenen Hoofd, Grasweg, the New Terminal, and NDSM all the way to the Hemhavens, and for which everyone simply pays: citizens, louts and foreigners, just like the vaporetti in Venice, with season tickets for locals and expensive day tickets for visitors.

I would not dare to steal their boat trip away from those romantics.

FERRY SERVICE AND BYCICLE SHED NEAR THE CENTRAL STATION

# MAPS

# OVERVIEW MAPS

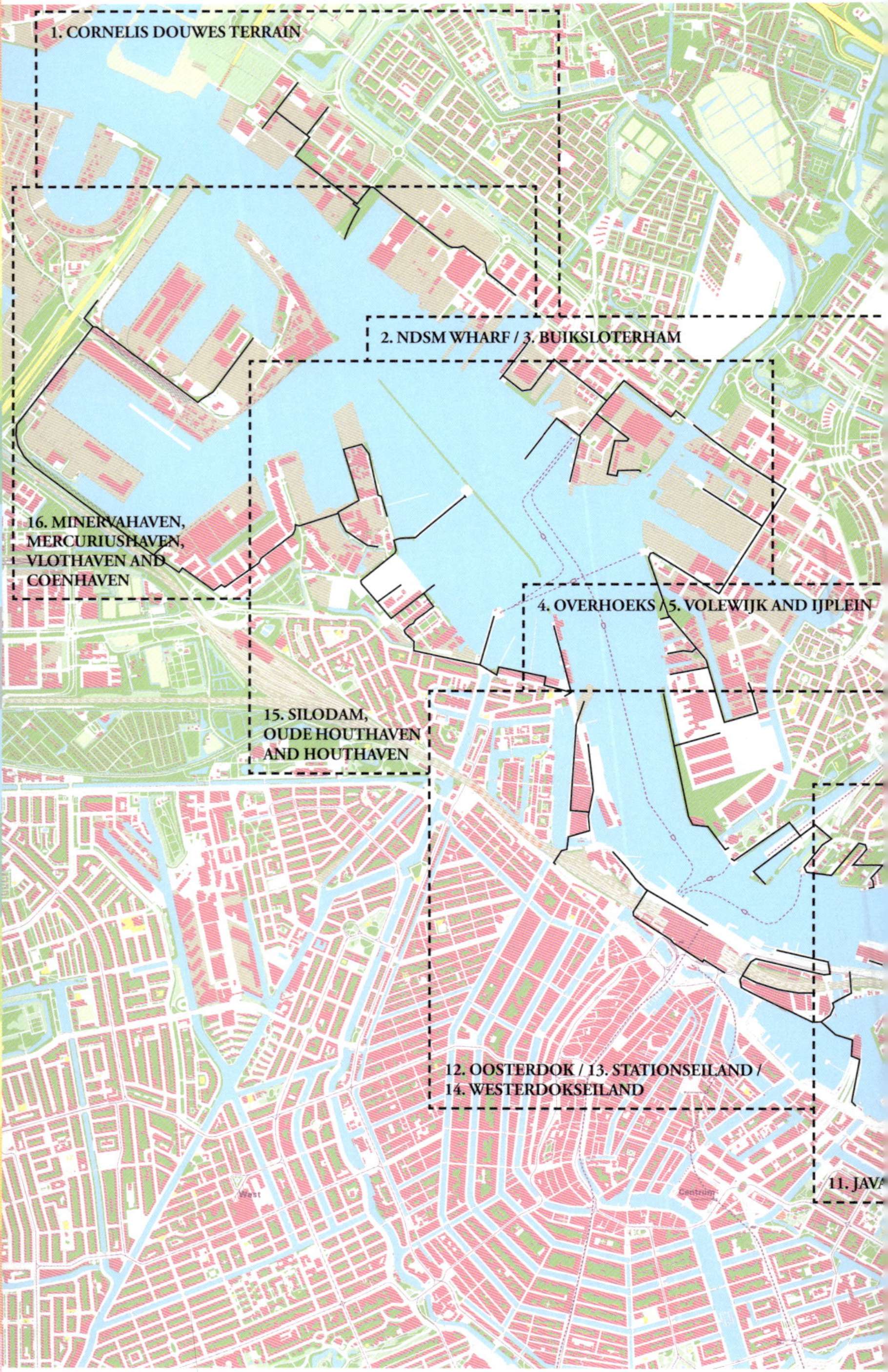

N
Noord
AMERSTRAAT DISTRICT /
IEUWENDAM
8. SCHELLINGWOUDE
PIET HEINKADE
9. ZEEBURGEREILAND / 10. ENTREPOT WEST,
BORNEO SPORENBURG AND KNSM ISLAND

VREDEWEG
ZIJKANAAL
A10
125P
NOORDZEEKANAAL
PROCESS
1.2
1.1
PETROLEUM-
HAVEN
-11.00
COENTUNNEL
-10.50
20
PETROLEUMHAVENWEG
COEN-
HAVEN
NOORDERHOOFD
PROPAANWEG
HEXAANWEG
PETROLEUMHAVENWEG
WESTERHOOFD
HAVENKOM A
AMERIKA
PIER
AFRIKA
PIER
HAVENKOM C
FOSFAATKADE
EINSTEINWEG
29
117P
A10
Pass.
Terminal
AZIE
COENHAVENWEG
COENHAVENWEG
PIER
PAPIERWEG
PIER EUROPA
FOSFAATKADE

TUINDORP
OOSTZAAN
HET IJ
CORNELIS
DOUWES-
KANAAL-WEST
KEER-
KRING-
PARK
WESTERTOCHT
OOSTERTOCHT
CORNELIS DOUWESWEG
COENTUNNELCIRCUIT
TT. VASUMWEG
HARDWAREWEG
PROGRAMMEUR-STRAAT
INTERNETSTRAAT
NETWERKWEG
ANALOOGSTRAAT
DIGITAALSTRAAT
BINAIRSTRAAT
SOFTWAREWEG
MONITORSTRAAT
PRINTERSTRAAT
COMPUTERWEG
SCANNERSTRAAT
MODEMSTRAAT
PLOTTERSTRAAT
TT. MELISSAWEG
DISKETTEWEG
TOETSENBORDWEG
KOMETENSINGEL
PLEJADENWEG
VEGASTRAAT
METEORENWEG
STELLINGWEG
KRAANSPOOR
NDSM-STRAAT
WERFSTRAAT
WERFKADE
MT. LINCOLNWEG
Dok 1
Dok 2
Dok 3
Dok 4
1.7
1.8
1.9
1.10
1.11
1.12
N

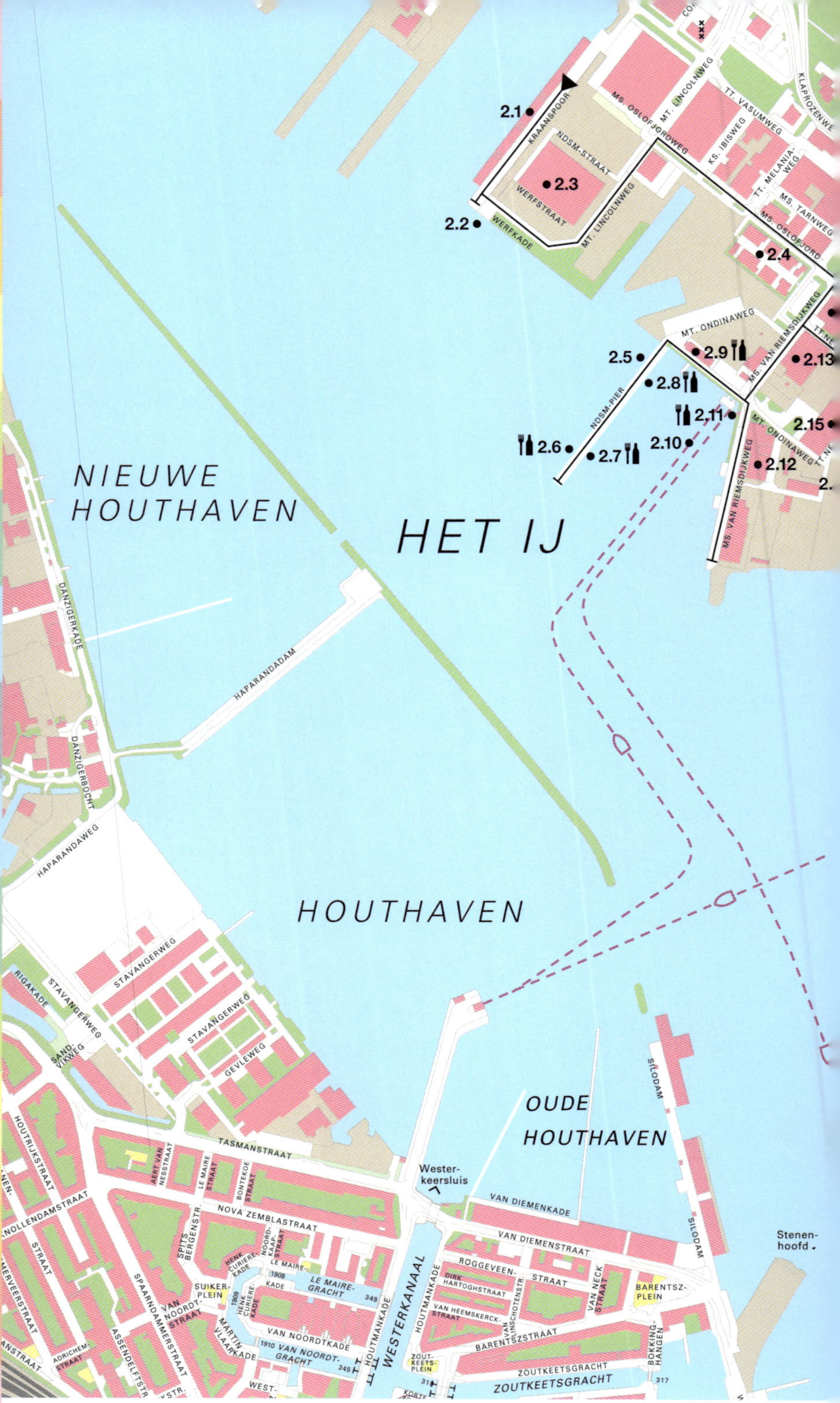

HET IJ
NIEUWE HOUTHAVEN
HOUTHAVEN
OUDE HOUTHAVEN
2.1
2.2
2.3
2.4
2.5
2.6
2.7
2.8
2.9
2.10
2.11
2.12
2.13
2.15
KRAANSPOOR
NDSM-STRAAT
WERFSTRAAT
WERFKADE
MT. LINCOLNWEG
MS. OSLOFJORDWEG
TT. VASUMWEG
KS. IBISWEG
TT. MELANIAWEG
MS. TARNWEG
MS. OSLOFJORD
KLAPROZENWEG
MT. ONDINAWEG
MS. VAN RIEMSDIJKWEG
NDSM-PIER
HAPARANDADAM
HAPARANDAWEG
DANZIGERKADE
DANZIGERBOCHT
RIGAKADE
STAVANGERWEG
SANDVIKWEG
GEVLEWEG
SILODAM
TASMANSTRAAT
Wester-keersluis
VAN DIEMENKADE
VAN DIEMENSTRAAT
Stenen-hoofd
HOUTRIJKSTRAAT
KNOLLENDAMSTRAAT
AERT VAN NESSTRAAT
LE MAIRE STRAAT
BONTEKOE STRAAT
NOVA ZEMBLASTRAAT
SPITSBERGENSTR.
HENK CURIËRE KADE
NOORD-KAAP-STRAAT
LE MAIRE KADE
LE MAIRE-GRACHT
SUIKER-PLEIN
SPAARNDAMMERSTRAAT
VAN NOORDT-STRAAT
MARTIN VLAARKADE
VAN NOORDTKADE
VAN NOORDT-GRACHT
ASSENDELFTSTR.
ADRICHEM-STRAAT
HOUTMANKADE
WESTERKANAAL
ROGGEVEEN-STRAAT
DIRK HARTOGHSTRAAT
VAN HEEMSKERCK-STRAAT
VAN LINSCHOTENSTR.
VAN NECK STRAAT
BARENTSZ-PLEIN
BARENTSZSTRAAT
ZOUT-KEETS-PLEIN
ZOUTKEETSGRACHT
BOKKING-HANGEN

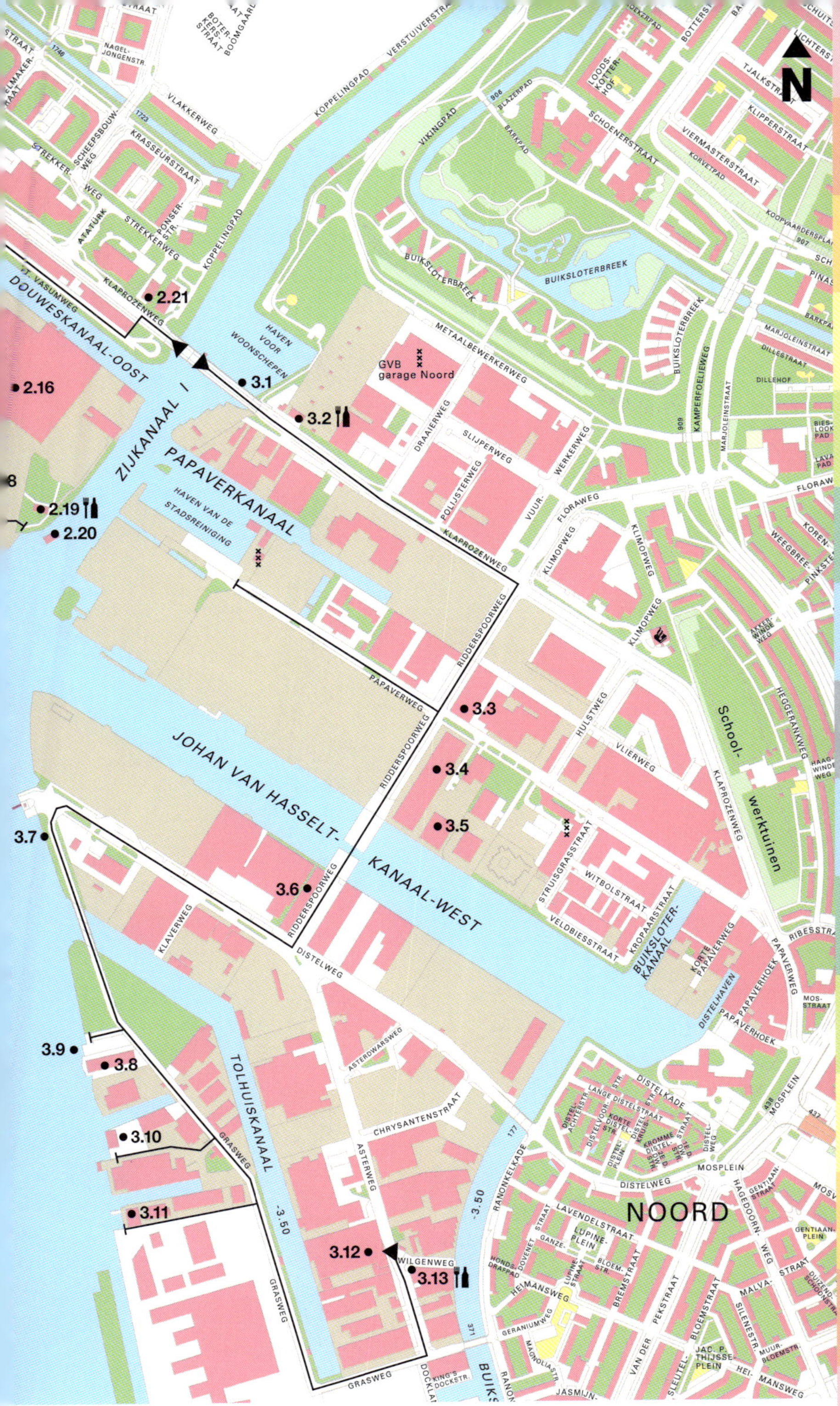
N
2.21
2.16
2.19
2.20
3.1
3.2
3.3
3.4
3.5
3.6
3.7
3.8
3.9
3.10
3.11
3.12
3.13
DOUWESKANAAL-OOST
ZIJKANAAL I
PAPAVERKANAAL
HAVEN VAN DE STADSREINIGING
HAVEN VOOR WOONSCHEPEN
GVB garage Noord
JOHAN VAN HASSELT-KANAAL-WEST
TOLHUISKANAAL
BUIKSLOTERKANAAL
DISTELHAVEN
BUIKSLOTERBREEK
School-werktuinen
NOORD
KLAPROZENWEG
RIDDERSPOORWEG
PAPAVERWEG
DISTELWEG
ASTERWEG
CHRYSANTENSTRAAT
GRASWEG
KLAVERWEG
WILGENWEG
METAALBEWERKERWEG
DRAAIERWEG
SLIJPERWEG
POLIJSTERWEG
VUURWERKERWEG
FLORAWEG
KLIMOPWEG
HULSTWEG
VLIERWEG
STRUISGRASSTRAAT
WITBOLSTRAAT
VELDBIESSTRAAT
KROPAARSTRAAT
PAPAVERHOEK
MOSPLEIN
RANONKELKADE
KOPPELINGPAD
VIKINGPAD
SCHOENERSTRAAT
VIERMASTERSTRAAT
KLIPPERSTRAAT
TJALKSTRAAT
KAMPERFOELIEWEG
MARJOLEINSTRAAT
HEGGERANKWEG
VLAKKERWEG
KRASSEURSTRAAT
STREKKERWEG
ATATURK
SCHEEPSBOUWWEG
VERSTUIVERSTRAAT
LAVENDELSTRAAT
HEIMANSWEG
GERANIUMWEG
BREMSTRAAT
PEKSTRAAT
VAN DER PEKSTRAAT
BLOEMSTRAAT
HAGEDOORNWEG
JAC. P. THIJSSE-PLEIN
KING'S DOCKSTR.
-3.50

DISTELWEG
ASTERDWARSWEG
CHRYSANTENSTRAAT
TOLHUISKANAAL
GRASWEG
ASTERWEG
-3.50
WILGENWEG
SILODAM
Stenen-
hoofd
BARENTSZ-
PLEIN
VAN NECK
STRAAT
BOKKING-
HANGEN
4.1
GRASWEG
KING'S
DOCKST
DOCKLANDSWEG
SAUSALITOLAAN
BUNDLAAN
SPADINALAAN
SPADINALAAN
KITSILANOSTRAAT
OVERHOEKSPARKLAAN
4.3
HAMMERBYSTRAAT
CÉRAMIQUELAAN
CÉRAMIQUELAAN
BERCYLAAN
WESTERDOKSDIJK
WESTERDOK
COFFIJ-
BOOM-
STRAAT
LELIENDAAL-
STRAAT
WINTHONT-
STRAAT
WESTERDOK
4.2
IJPROMENADE
BERCYLAAN
LIDO-
PLEIN
TOLHUISWEG
4.6
BADHUISKADE
4.4
OVERHOEKS-
PLEIN
IJPROMENADE
4.5
4.7
4.8
5.2
OVERHOEKS
BUIKSLOTERW
5.1
VOORHAVEN VAN
NOORDHOLLAN
5.7
WESTERDOKS
PLEIN
Westerdok-
sluis
WESTER-
DOKSKADE
DE RUIJTERKADE
WESTER-
TOEGANG
ZANDHOEK
TAAN-
STR.
GRACHT
NGRACHT
WESTERDOK
GROTE BICKERSSTR.
HOLLANDSE TUIN
ZEIL-
MAKERSTR.
BLOK-
MAKERSTR.
KETEL-
MAKERSTR.
HAARLEMMER
NIEUWE WESTERDOKSTRAAT
HOUTTUINEN
HAARLEMMER-
STRAAT
BROUWERS-
GRACHT
HEREN-
MARKT
DROOGBAK
DROOGBAK
STATIONSPLEIN
OPEN
PRINS HENDRIKKADE
DE RUIJTERKADE
Centraal Station
Centraal Station
OOSTER-
TOEGANG
HAVEN-
STATIONSPLEIN
FRONT
PRINS HENDRIKKADE
OOSTERDOKSSTR.
KEIZERSGRACHT
HERENGRACHT
SINGEL
SINGEL
LANGESTRAAT
STROMARKT
KATTENGAT
NIEUWENDIJK
MARTELAARS-
GRACHT
HEKELVELD
NZ. ARMSTG.
OUDE BRAAK
ST JACOBSSTR.

N
FLORAPARK
VOLEWIJKS-PARK
NOORDHOLLANDSCH KANAAL
NOORD
HET IJ
IJ-TUNNEL
MOTORKANAAL
NIEUWE LEEUWARDERWEG
LEEUWARDERWEG
JOHAN VAN HASSELTWEG
BUIKSLOTERWEG
MOSPLEIN
MOSVELD
DISTELWEG
DISTELKADE
PAPAVERWEG
PAPAVERHOEK
RIBESSTRAAT
BERBERISSTRAAT
WINGERDWEG
HAGEDOORNWEG
HAGEDOORNPLEIN
VARENWEG
BLOEMSTRAAT
VAN DER PEKSTRAAT
MEIDOORNWEG
JAC. P. THIJSSE-PLEIN
PLEIN SPANJE '36-'39
KRAAIENPLEIN
ADELAARSWEG
MERELSTR.
PLUVIERPLEIN
KALKOENSTR.
MEEUWENPLEIN
ALBATROSPAD
FAZANTENWEG
KWARTELSTR.
ZWANENPLEIN
MEZENSTRAAT
MEEUWENLAAN
SCHAAFSTRAAT
BEITELKADE
SPIJKERKADE
HAMERSTRAAT
MOTORKADE
GEDEMPT HAMERKANAAL
KETELSTRAAT
BOORSTRAAT
MOTORWAL
KETELMAKERIJ
BANKWERKERIJ
HET DOK
NOORDWAL
SPREEUWENPARK
NACHTEGAALSTRAAT
SPERWERLAAN
HAVIKSLAAN
ZWALUWSTR.
LEEUWERIKSTRAAT
VALKENWEG
SIXHAVENWEG
MEEUWENLAAN
IJPLEIN
PONTPLEIN
HOLLANDIA KATTENBURGPAD
GEDEMPTE инсте
5.4
5.9
5.10
5.12
5.13
-0.40
SUMATRAKADE
JAVAKADE
TOSARISTRAAT
TOSARI-TUIN
BRANTASGRACHT
Jan Schaeferbrug
VEEMKADE
Passagiers-terminal
PIET HEINKADE
JOLLEMANHOF
VEEMBROEDERHOF

FLORAPARK
VOLEWIJKSPARK
NOORDHOLLANDSCH KANAAL
W.H. VLIEGENBOS
-0.70
Kampeerterrein
Volkstuinenpark Buitenzorg
6.1
6.2
6.3
6.4
6.5
6.6
6.7
6.8
6.9
6.10
6.11
6.12
6.13
6.14
6.15
7.1
MOTORKANAAL
PONTHAVEN
JOHAN VAN HASSELT-KANAAL-OOST
IJHAVEN
Jan Schaeferbrug
SUMATRAKADE
JAVAKADE
VEEMKADE
NIEUWENDAMMERDIJK
JOHAN VAN HASSELTWEG
GEDEMPT HAMERKANAAL
HAMERSTRAAT
SCHAAFSTRAAT
MOKERSTR.
AAMBEELDSTR.
KETELSTRAAT
BOORSTRAAT
ZAMENHOFSTRAAT

N
-1.50
WATERGANGSEWEG
PURMERWEG
PURMERPLEIN
NIEUWENDAMMERDIJK
VOLENDAMMERWEG
MONNIKENDAMMERWEG
EDAMMERSTRAAT
BEEMSTERSTRAAT
WERENGOUW
KOEDIJKPAD
SCHOORLSTRAAT
DE EGMONDENSTRAAT
GROTE DIESTRAAT
KLEINE DIESTR.
MEDEMBLIKSTR.
HOORNSESTR.
DAMMERDIJK
EREBOOMSLOOT
NIEUWENDAMMERKADE
7.4
GROTE HAVEN
7.5
7.6
-0.30
7.7
7.8
7.9
7.9
ZIJKANAAL K NAAR NIEUWENDAM
-4.00
SCHELLING-WOUDER-BREEK
HET IJ
SURINAMEKADE
KNSM - LAAN
BARCELONA-PLEIN
PIRAEUS-PLEIN
LEVANT-PLEIN
LEVANTKADE
VENETIËHOF
RIJNLOODSPAD

SCHELLINGWOUDERDIJK
Sportpark Schellingwoude
-1.50
8.1
HOYERPAD
BAVINCKHOF
NOORDERIJDIJK
Oranjesluizen
8.2
8.3
HET IJ
Prins Willem Alexandersluis
ZUIDER IJDIJK
SURINAMEKADE
VENETIËHOF
RIJNLOODSPAD
MOND VAN HET AMSTERDAM-RIJNKANAAL
Piet Heintunnel
PIET HEINTUNNEL
IJBURGLAAN
ZUIDERZEEWEG
Eiland
-0.40
VAN HENGELSTRAAT
LAMPENISTENSTRAAT
P.E. TEGELBERGPLEIN
PLANTSOEN
POMPMANSTRAAT
SCHEEPSTIMMERMANSTRAAT
BOTTELIERPLEIN
BINNENHAVEN
STOKERKADE
BOOTSMANSTRAAT
BORNEOKADE
CRUQUIUSWEG

Volkstuinenpark
Tuinwijck
-1.80
Volkstuinenpark
Rust en Vreugd
-1.80
Volkstuinenpark
Kweeklust
-1.80
ZUIDERZEEWEG
ZWARTEGOUW
LIERGOUW
PATERSLAAN
A 10
RINGWEG-NOORD
DURGERDAMMERDIJK
SCHELLINGWOUDERDIJK
KLEISLOOT
8.7
8.6
8.8
Schellingwouderbrug
Blauwe Hoofd
IJBURGLAAN
ZUIDER-IJSTRAAT
N

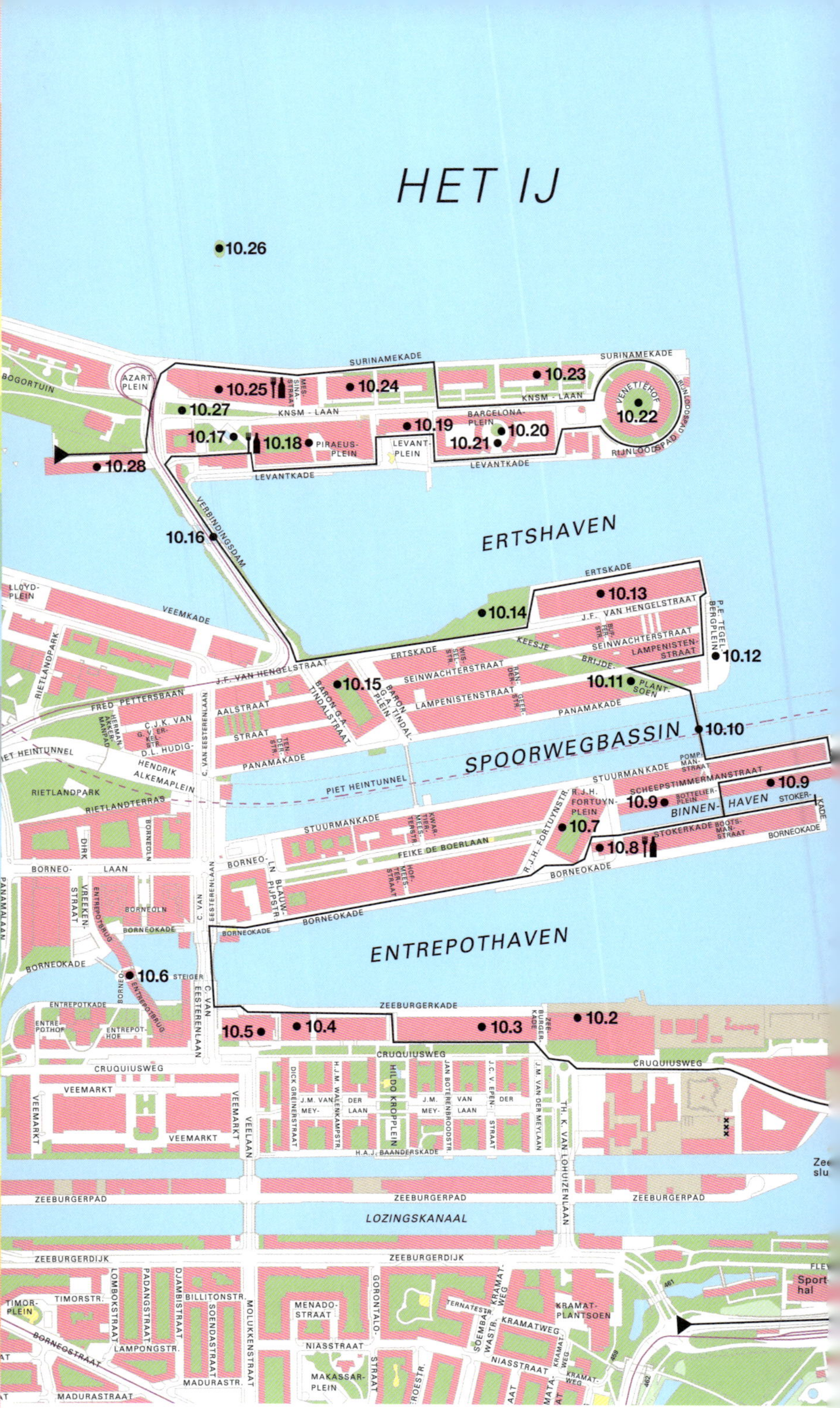
HET IJ
ERTSHAVEN
SPOORWEGBASSIN
ENTREPOTHAVEN
LOZINGSKANAAL
BINNEN-HAVEN
10.26
10.25
10.24
10.23
10.22
10.27
10.19
10.20
10.21
10.17
10.18
10.28
10.16
10.13
10.14
10.12
10.15
10.11
10.10
10.9
10.9
10.7
10.8
10.6
10.5
10.4
10.3
10.2
SURINAMEKADE
KNSM - LAAN
LEVANTKADE
VERBINDINGSDAM
ERTSKADE
J.F. VAN HENGELSTRAAT
SEINWACHTERSTRAAT
LAMPENISTENSTRAAT
PANAMAKADE
STUURMANKADE
FEIKE DE BOERLAAN
BORNEOKADE
BORNEOLAAN
ZEEBURGERKADE
CRUQUIUSWEG
VEEMARKT
ZEEBURGERPAD
ZEEBURGERDIJK
RIETLANDPARK
VEEMKADE
PIET HEINTUNNEL
ENTREPOTKADE
VEELAAN
C. VAN EESTERENLAAN
TH. K. VAN LOHUIZENLAAN
BORNEOSTRAAT
MADURASTRAAT
NIASSTRAAT
KRAMATWEG
MOLUKKENSTRAAT

N
Prins Willem Alexandersluis
LIERGOUW
ZUIDERZEEWEG
SCHELLINGWOUD
Schellingwouderbrug
ZUIDER IJDIJK
MOND VAN HET AMSTERDAM-RIJNKANAAL
Eiland Zeeburg
9.2
-0.40
9.1
tunnel
9.3
PIET HEINTUNNEL
IJBURGLAAN
9.5
9.4
CRUQUIUSWEG
ZUIDER IJDIJK
SYPHONSLUIS
VOORBOEZEM
9.8
Amsterdamse-brug
9.6
9.7
Camping Zeeburg

IJHAVEN
Jan Schaeferbrug
SUMATRAKADE
JAVAKADE
VEEMKADE
PIET HEINKADE
Passagiers-terminal
DIJKSGRACHT
Mariniersbrug
Marine Etablissement
Nemo
Scheepvaart-museum
Kattenburgerbrug
NIEUWE VAART
Pelikaanbrug
MOTORKANAAL
OOSTENBURGERVAART
WITTENBURGERVAART
KATTENBURGER-VAART
ENTREPOTDOK
OOSTERDOK
11.4
11.5
11.6
11.7
11.8
11.19
11.20
11.21
11.22
11.23
11.24
11.25
11.26
11.27
11.28
11.29
11.30
11.31
11.32
11.33
11.34
11.35

N
JOHAN VAN HASSELT-KANAAL-OOST
HET IJ
SUMATRAKADE
KRATON-TUIN
JAVAKADE
MAJANG-GRACHT
SERANG-GRACHT
BOGORTUIN
AZARTPLEIN
11.1
11.2
11.3
11.5
11.5
SURINAMEKADE
KNSM - LAAN
KNSM - LAAN
MESSINASTRAAT
BARCELONA-PLEIN
PIRAEUS-PLEIN
LEVANT-PLEIN
LEVANTKADE
LEVANTKADE
VERBINDINGSDAM
ERTSHAVEN
VEEMKADE
VEEMKADE
OOSTELIJKE HANDELSKADE
LLOYD-PLEIN
PIET HEINKADE
RIETLANDPARK
11.9
11.10
11.11
11.12
11.13
11.14
11.15
11.16
J.F. VAN HENGELSTRAAT
ERTSKADE
KEESJE
SEINWACHTERSTRAAT
LAMPENISTENSTRAAT
BARON G.A. TINDALSTRAAT
BARON G.A. TINDAL-PLEIN
FRED. PETTERSBAAN
AALSTRAAT
STRAAT
PANAMAKADE
PANAMAK
C.J.K. VAN
D.L. HUDIG-
HENDRIK ALKEMAPLEIN
C. VAN EESTERENLAAN
PIET HEINTUNNEL
PIET HEINTUNNEL
SPOORWEGBASSIN
RIETLANDPARK
RIETLANDTERRAS
STUURMANKADE
FEIKE DE BOERLAAN
R.J.H. FORTUYNPLEIN
R.J.H. FORTUYNSTR.
BORNEO-LAAN
BORNEO-
BORNEOKADE
BORNEOKADE
BORNEOKADE
BORNEOKADE
BORNEOLN
DIRK VREEKENSTRAAT
ENTREPOTBRUG
STEIGER
ENTREPOTKADE
ENTREPOTHOF
ZEEBURGERKADE
CRUQUIUSWEG
CRUQUIUSWEG
VEEMARKT
VEEMARKT
VEEMARKT
PANAMALAAN
PANAMALAAN
DIJKSGRACHT
VAN REEDESTRAAT
RUMPHIUSSTR.
CONRADSTRAAT
BLANKENSTRAAT
PETERSTRAAT
LEEGHWATERSTR.
FRANS DE WOLLANTSTRAAT
FUNENPARK
KEERWAL
HILDO KROPPLEIN
DICK GREINERSTRAAT
H.J.M. WALENKAMPSTR.
JAN BOTERENBROODSTR.
J.M. VAN DER MEYLAAN

14.11
14.10
14.7
14.9
14.8
14.6
14.5
14.3
14.4
14.2
14.1
13.11
13.10
13
WESTERDOK
WESTERDOKSDIJK
COFFIJ-BOOM-STRAAT
LELIENDAAL-STRAAT
WINTHONT-STRAAT
WESTERDOKSPLEIN
Westerdok-sluis
WESTER-DOKSKADE
DE RUIJTERKADE
HE
ZOUTKEETSGRACHT
REALENGRACHT
BARENTSZSTRAAT
VAN NOORDTKADE
VAN NOORDTGRACHT
VIERWINDENSTRAAT
PRINSENEILAND
BICKERSGRACHT
GROTE BICKERSSTR.
HOLLANDSE TUIN
TUSSEN DE BOGEN
EILANDSGRACHT
HAARLEMMER HOUTTUINEN
NIEUWE WESTERDOKSTRAAT
HAARLEMMERDIJK
HAARLEMMERSTRAAT
HAARLEMMERPLEIN
NASSAUPLEIN
WITTENKADE
NASSAUKADE
MARNIXSTRAAT
SINGELGRACHT
LIJNBAANSGRACHT
BROUWERSGRACHT
PRINSENGRACHT
KEIZERSGRACHT
HERENGRACHT
SINGEL
PALMGRACHT
PALMSTRAAT
WILLEMSSTRAAT
GOUDSBLOEMSTRAAT
LINDENGRACHT
LINDENSTRAAT
NOORDERMARKT
HERENMARKT
WESTERSTRAAT
ANJELIERSSTRAAT
TUINSTRAAT
EGELANTIERSSTRAAT
EGELANTIERSGRACHT
LELIEGRACHT
NIEUWE LELIESTRAAT
BLOEMGRACHT
BLOEMSTRAAT
ROZENGRACHT
ROZENSTRAAT
LAURIERSTRAAT
LAURIERGRACHT
REESTRAAT
HARTENSTRAAT
WESTERMARKT
Westerkerk
RAADHUISSTRAAT
PRINSENSTR.
HERENSTRAAT
OUDE LELIESTRAAT
DRIEKONINGENSTRAAT
NIEUWEZIJDS VOORBURGWAL
SPUISTRAAT
Nieuwe Kerk
Koninklijk Paleis
DAM
PALEISSTR.
BEURSPLEIN
DAMRAK
WARMOESSTRAAT
DAMSTRAAT
DROOGBAK
PRINS
STROMARKT
KATTENGAT
HEKELVELD
EERSTE MARNIXPLANTSOEN
MARNIXPLEIN
DOMELA NIEUWENHUISPLANTSOEN

N
GERANIUMWEG
MAGNOLIASTR.
JASMIJN-
OLEANDER-
ANEMOON-
VAN DER PEK-
STRAAT
SLEUTEL-
BLOEMS
JAC. P. THIJSSE-PLEIN
MEIDOORN-PLEIN
MEIDOORNWEG
MUURBLOEMSTR.
HEI-
MANSWEG
WINGERD
HAGEDOORNPLEIN
PLEIN SPANJE '36-'39
BEGONIASTRAAT
VAN DER PEKPLEIN
LAANWEG
-0.40
BUIKSLOTERWEG
KRAAIENPLEIN
GRASWEG
DOCKLANDSWEG
KING'S DOCKSTR.
BUIKSLOTERKANAAL
RANONKELKADE
BUNDLAAN
SAUSALITOLAAN
SPADINALAAN
PRINCES DOCK-STRAAT
KITSILANOSTRAAT
HAMMERBYSTRAAT
CÉRAMIQUELAAN
BERCYLAAN
BADHUISKADE
OVERHOEKSPARKLAAN
IJPROMENADE
LIDO-PLEIN
TOLHUISWEG
OVERHOEKS-PLEIN
OVERHOEKS
Willem I
VOORHAVEN VAN HET NOORDHOLLANDSCH KANAAL
(Noord-Zuidlijn in aanleg)
SIXHAVENWEG
SIXHAVEN
VOORMALIGE SCHUTSLUIS WILLEM III
MEEUWENLAAN
IJ-TUNNEL
1942
ADELAARSWEG
REIGERWEG
NACHTEGAALSTRAAT
SPERWERLAAN
SPREEUWENPARK
OOIEVAARSWEG
VALKENWEG
INSTEEKHAVEN
IJPLEIN
PONT-PLEIN
HOLLANDIA KATTENBURGPAD
GEDEMPTE
GIETERIJ
SMEDERIJ
KOPER-SLAGERIJ
13.8
13.7
DE RUIJTERKADE
13.5
Centraal Station
13.3
STATIONSPLEIN
OOSTERTOEGANG
486
13.2
13.1
FRONT
PRINS HENDRIKKADE
12.12
12.14
12.15
12.16
12.17
12.18
12.19
12.1
12.2
12.3
485
PIET HEINKADE
Passagiersterminal
OOSTERDOKSTR.
12.13
12.11
SIMON CARMIGGELTSTRAAT
HARRY BANNINKSTR.
WILLEM FREDERIK HERMANSSTR.
12.9
12.8
ANNIE M.G. SCHMIDTSTRAAT
DOORGANG
OOSTERDOKS-
12.10
OOSTERDOKSKADE
12.4
Nemo
12.5
OOSTER-
DOK
IJ-TUNNEL
OOSTERDOK
12.6
Scheepvaart-museum
12.7
Kattenburg
1941
PRINS HENDRIKKADE
KALKMARKT
'S-GRAVENHEKJE
PEPERSTRAAT
RAPENBURG
SCHANS
OUDE SCHANS
BUITEN BANTAMMERSTRAAT
BINNENKANT
SCHIPPERSSTRAAT
EILANDSGRACHT
OUDE WAAL
WAALS
KROMME WAAL
GELDERSEKADE
ZEEDIJK
OUDEZIJDS KOLK
NIEUWE BRUGSTEEG
OUDEZIJDS VOORBURGWAL
WAALSTEEG
BINNEN BANTAMMERSTR.
RECHTBOOMSSLOOT
JONKERSTR.
RIDDERSTRAAT
KONINGSSTRAAT
MONTELBAANSTRAAT
KROMBOOMSSLOOT
Waag
NIEUWMARKT
Nieuwmarkt
MONNIKENSTR.
BLOEDSTRAAT
BARNDESTEEG
MOLENSTEEG
STORMSTEEG

MINERVA-HAVEN
NIEUWE HOUTHAVEN
HOUTHA
MINERVAHAVENWEG
DANZIGERKADE
HOUTVEEMKANAAL
ARCHANGELKADE
DANZIGERBOCHT
RIGAKADE
HAPARANDADAM
HAPARANDAWEG
15.14
15.15
15.13
15.12
15.9
15.11
15.10
15.7
STAVANGERWEG
GEVLEWEG
SANDVIKWEG
TASMANSTRAAT
Volkstuinenpark Zonnehoek
ARCHANGELWEG
SPAARNDAMMERDIJK
POLANENHOF
Brediusbad
ZAANDAMMERPLEIN
Sporthal
ZAANHOF
KOOGSTRAAT
HEMBRUGSTRAAT
OOSTZAANSTRAAT
HOUTRIJKSTRAAT
POLANENSTRAAT
KNOLLENDAMSTRAAT
SPAARNDAMMERPLANTSOEN
WORMERVEERSTRAAT
ZAANSTRAAT
ADRICHEMSTRAAT
ASSENDELFTSTR.
SPAARNDAMMERSTRAAT
ZAANDIJKSTR.
AERT VAN NESSTRAAT
LE MAIRESTRAAT
BONTEKOESTRAAT
NOVA ZEMBLASTRAAT
SPITSBERGENSTR.
SUIKERPLEIN
VAN NOORDTSTRAAT
MARTIN VLAARKADE
LE MAIREGRACHT
VAN NOORDTKADE
VAN NOORDTGRACHT
HOUTMANKADE
WESTERKANAAL
WESTZAANSTRAAT
DOMELA NIEUWENHUIS PLANTSOEN
MANKADE
WESTERPARK
KLÖNNE PLEIN
GOSSCHALKLAAN
PAZZANISTRAAT
Stadsdeelkantoor
-0.55

N
HET IJ
MT. LINCOLNWEG
MS. TARNWEG
MS. OSLOFJORD
MS. VAN RIEMSDIJKWEG
MT. ONDINAWEG
MS. VAN RIEMSDIJKWEG
TT. NEVERITAWEG
NDSM-PIER
MT. ONDINAWEG
TT. NEVERITAWEG
MS. VAN RIEMSDIJKWEG
CORN. DOUWESKANAAL-OOST
TT. VASUMWEG
ATATÜRK
STREKKERWEG
PONSER-STR.
KLAPROZENWEG
KOPPELINGPAD
HAVEN VOOR WOONSCHEPEN
GVB garage Noord
DRAAIERWEG
ZIJKANAAL I
PAPAVERKANAAL
HAVEN VAN DE STADSREINIGING
PAPAVERWEG
RIDDERSPOORWEG
RIDDERSPOORWEG
KLAVERWEG
DISTELWEG
ASTERDWARSWEG
CHRYSANTENSTR.
TOLHUISKANAAL
-3.50
GRASWEG
ASTERWEG
WILGENWEG
GRASWEG
GRASWEG
DOCKLANDSWEG
SAUSALITOLAAN
BUNDLAAN
SPADINALAAN
SPADINALAAN
KITSILANOSTRAAT
HAMMERBYSTRAAT
CÉRAMIQUELAAN
OVERHOEKSPARKLAAN
SILODAM
15.4
OUDE HOUTHAVEN
15.3
SILODAM
15.2
Stenen-hoofd
15.5
BARENTSZ-PLEIN
15.1
VAN NECK STRAAT
BOKKING-HANGEN
317
ZANDHOEK
TAAN-STR.
JAN MENG-PLEIN
316
WESTERDOK
WESTERDOKSDIJK
COFFIJ-BOOM-STRAAT

-10.50
PETROLEUMHAVENWEG
VAN RIEBEECKHAVENWEG
BUTAANWEG
PROPAANWEG
PETROLEUMHAVENWEG
HEXAANWEG
COEN-
HAVEN
16.10
HAVENKOM A
WESTERHOOFD
EINSTEINWEG
A10
117P
29
PIER
AMERIKA
PIER
AFRIKA
HAVENKOM C
16.9
Pass.
Terminal
COENHAVENWEG
COENHAVENWEG
AZIE
PIER
PAPIERWEG
PIER EUROPA
FOSFAATKADE
VLOTHAVENWEG
VLOTHAVEN
16.8
MERC
388
VLOTHAVENWEG
361
NEPTUNUSHAVEN
-10.50
NIEUWE HEMWEG
16.7
STRAAT
CONTACTWEG
-0.40
Isolatorweg
GENERATORSTRAAT
16.6

N
CORNELIS DOUWES-KANAAL-WEST
INTERNETSTRAAT
ANALOOGSTRAAT
DIGITAALSTRAAT
NETWERKWEG
BINAIRSTRAAT
TT. VASUMWEG
SOFTWAREWEG
MONITORSTRAAT
PRINTERSTRAAT
SCANNERSTRAAT
TT. MELISSAWEG
Dok 1
Dok 2
Dok 3
Dok 4
KRAANSPOOR
WERFSTRAAT
WERFKADE
HET IJ
MINERVA-HAVEN
NIEUWE HOUTHAVEN
MINERVAHAVENWEG
DANZIGERKADE
16.1
16.2
16.3
16.4
16.5
ARCHANGELKADE
DANZIGERBOCHT
RIGAKADE
HAPARANDADAM
HAPARANDAWEG
HOUTHAVEN

MAARTEN KLOOS

# WATERFRONT IN THE SUN

With every one of its pores orientated towards the ocean in the West, Los Angeles has its Sunset Boulevard where the evening is celebrated. In Barcelona the Avinguda del Paral-lel has the same precise East-West orientation, though the intention here is to dramatically anchor the city to the rising of the sun. These are two examples of the linking of the city and city life to the source of life on earth, the sun. The designers of the IJ waterfront do not seem to have paid much attention to this aspect, but there are still many points of contact.

## NORTH AMSTERDAM

In 1988 the Spatial Planning department of the newly created North Amsterdam District published a memorandum on the 10-kilometre stretch along the North Bank of the IJ. That memorandum invited the policymakers involved to choose between a future scenario in which the IJ would continue to be the boundary between a metropolitan city centre and a more rural North Amsterdam, on the one hand, and the concept in which the IJ could form the link between two more equal areas, on the other hand. The choice fell on the latter, as a result of which the IJ has assumed a completely different significance from what it had before. What at that moment was still regarded as the northern waterfront of the city became the South Bank of the IJ, and from now on the southern bank of 'the other side' (North Amsterdam) became the North Bank of the IJ. The River IJ itself, that had always been the water north of the city (centre), increasingly became a spatial element with a position in the centre. In the subsequent developments every possible aspect of relevance to the relation between the city centre and North Amsterdam has been given consideration except – remarkably enough – the significance that the sun gives to the notions of north and south. This blind spot is not new in urban planning, nor is it inexplicable; it is based on the fact that individuals too often do not know how to deal properly with the sun. After all, the best way to benefit from the energy of the sun is to face it, but you can only see something of the world if you turn your back to the sun. As an extension of that, the rule for urban planners and architects is: buildings in the sun insulate themselves to a certain extent. They are easy to see, but they do not look back. As a result, the desire to catch daylight has dominated the development of urban design in a rather clumsy way down to the present.

## RIVER IJ

Thinking in terms of the southern and northern banks of the IJ might be taken to imply: there is more eye-catching light in the north, so that is where there should be a deliberate attempt to create the best possible architecture that also manifests itself from a distance. The main quality of the south, on the other hand, is that the southern bank of the IJ affords a splendid view of the architecture of North Amsterdam. However, the situation is not as simple as it seems. From the A10 ring road in the West to the NDSM terrain the IJ runs in a southeasterly/northwesterly direction; it follows a course that is practically North-South at Silodam/Westerdokseiland and Buiksloterham; the only real East-West stretch is that from Overhoeks/Central Station to the A10 ring road in the East. With regard to orientation towards the sun, one might therefore expect an approach aimed at expressing this tripartite division in the programme and architecture. Yet such an approach is by no means visible everywhere.

In the eastern basin there are long south-facing façades on the southern bank of the IJ that are visible from the city centre and that for the most part possess the quality that they deserve. Here the corresponding façades facing north have sometimes also really been put in the shade. The Java island is good in this respect, but awareness of this aspect had not completely taken hold in the (earlier) buildings of the KNSM island, except in the case of the architects of the low, elongated block of apartments on the northern side. On the Oosterdokseiland the extreme variation on the southern side is relevant, but a much calmer look would have been more in place on the side facing north. Of course it is interesting to see what the plans for the easternmost riverbank in North Amsterdam will be.

In the western basin too, it is questionable whether the plans for North Amsterdam will properly take into account the fact that everything that is built beside the water here will profit outstandingly from the sun. If there is one location where the programme of the buildings ought to have some connection with the sun and a high architectural quality, it is here. So far, however, the results have been disappointing. Even in the case of the Kraanspoor, that is stunning in many ways, it can be said that its function should have been related more closely to the specific qualities of the location. In every respect there are good grounds for expecting something better from the future plans for the NDSM terrain.

The area in between, where the so-called North Bank of the IJ is actually an eastern one, and where the so-called South Bank of the IJ is actually a western one, poses a major challenge in terms of orientation towards the sun, but here too the principals and designers have not yet shown themselves to be sufficiently aware of the fact. The apartments with terraces in Overhoeks make good use of the sun, but could have been much more interesting architecturally. The Filmmuseum, on the other hand, is of a high architectural quality, but its programme did not necessarily require it to be located on this spot. The laying out of a green riverbank is perfectly in place here. The further future plans for Buiksloterham will have to score on all fronts.

## UNDERESTIMATION

Generally speaking, we may conclude that the significance of the sun has been considerably underestimated so far. Shell and HEMA have erected buildings on tremendously attractive and prestigious locations which are of no use to the people of Amsterdam; the building of more of this category of sombre-looking prestige projects should be avoided. In the case of the glass volumes of the Muziekgebouw and Kraanspoor, the question has to be raised of whether buildings that primarily offer an interesting view should have been kept so open. As for the public domain, one has the impression that the various beaches are almost without exception on the wrong side of the IJ. And with a view to the completion of the Central Station, there is reason to hold one's breath to see whether what was once the rear of the station will be successfully turned into a fully fledged second front, with a façade that is recognisable as such for the increasing flow of people who will flock to it from North Amsterdam – with the sun in their eyes!

# 9. ZEEBURGEREILAND

At the end of the nineteenth century the Ministry of Public Works created an embankment here, followed by another at right angles to it later, to prevent the silting up of the channel between the IJmeer and the Oranjesluizen as much as possible. This resulted in a triangular area of water in which dredgings could be kept. An increasingly large part of it found itself above the water level and the Zeeburgereiland was a fact.
The Schellingwoude Naval Airfield was located on the northern side between 1916 and 1948. The Dutch Royal Navy also had a Morse transmitter there. During the Second World War the occupying forces operated from the airfield. After the war the island was given a mixed function. A naval hospital was established there that was also used for civilians because of the shortage of hospitals in Amsterdam. Around 1960 the idea was briefly mooted of transferring the entire operations of the naval base on Kattenburg to the Zeeburgereiland.
The Amsterdam Municipal Police used the island as a depot for tuned up motorbikes, but it was easy to recover parts because of the lack of surveillance. The University of Amsterdam had laboratories for plant physiology and neural research on the Zuider IJdijk. This fringe within the A10 ring road also accommodated dog owners' associations, a riding school, an allotment complex, housing for refugees, a rock 'n' roll clubhouse, building firms, garages and many artists. The majority of these users had to leave because of the building plans for the island.
For a long time the main function of the island was the sewage purification plant for East Amsterdam that was opened there in 1982. It was the largest in the Netherlands at the time. Its operations put an end to the many years of the discharging of untreated sewage into the Buiten IJ. Zeeburg was an ideal location in the past as it was far from the city and the problem of bad smells did not seem to matter there. With the plans for IJburg, and in the light of the stricter purification criteria imposed by the EU, it was decided to move the plant westwards.
Given the location of the Zeeburgereiland between the eastern area of the docks and IJburg, it seems a natural development to turn it into a residential and work area with 5,500 homes and related facilities. The planning stage is largely complete, but the economic crisis is causing part of its implementation to stagnate. The first planned residential zone with a business strip, RI-Oost, is in the north-eastern corner of the island, which has been divided into four. To prevent the history of the site from disappearing, three silos and two houses belonging to the former plants are being preserved. The other three parts of the island are being given a temporary function for the time being. The new student accommodation in the south-eastern corner is a part of this policy.

## 9.1 WAAIDORP / ANNIE M.G. SCHMIDT HOUSE

**Address:** IJburglaan
**Architect:** Arons en Gelauff Architecten, ThisisJane Interieurontwerp
**Client:** AM / de Alliantie
**Year:** 2011 / 2015

'There is dance, there is film, a theatre, a library, a reading room. And that is unique in the Netherlands. These were the words of Annie M.G. Schmidt, the famous author of children's book, two years before her death when she heard about the first plans for the Annie M.G. Schmidt House. It was only many years later that it proved possible to find a location for this initiative with the winning entry in a competition organised by the local authority to come up with a function for two of the three silos of the former East Amsterdam sewage purification plant.
A playground will be constructed on the roof of one of the silos, and the restaurant Praq op 't daq, on the roof of the other. A transparent intermediate volume will connect the two silos. The ground floor will accommodate a café, a shop, and a theatre that can be opened up for open air performances. Until the renovation of the silos is complete there will be a temporary facility, with activities that show what the Annie M.G. Schmidt House will have to offer in the future.

*There is still something of the feeling of being on the fringe of a big city beside the Zuider IJdijk with its old lock houses on the dyke and various sheds and barracks with all kinds of functions. There are car firms, artists and a small riding school. Temporary accommodation for refugees is now in use by students. One of the sheds accommodates the artists who had to leave the Westerdoks island earlier. The south-western corner is the domain of the community that sprang up around the artist Theo Niermeyer (1940–2005). He was known as the Iron Poet because of the recycling of steel and iron in his work. The terrain is still full of his work.*

## 9.2 ZEEBURGEREILAND PUMP STATION

**Address:** Zuiderzeeweg
**Architect:** Bekkering Adams Architecten
**Client:** Dienst Waterbeheer en Riolering
**Year:** 2005

Besides the silos, there is little of the history of the sewage purification plant to be seen. As on the Klaprozenweg in North Amsterdam, there is now a booster pump station here to collect sewage from East Amsterdam and pump it on to the purification plant in the western area of the docks.
The main function of this specially designed building is to hide the pump from sight and to reduce noise. The prefabricated sand-blasted concrete skin is formed around the functional elements of the plant. The roof has also been designed as a fully-fledged part of the many-sided object. The ornaments beneath the overhangs cast a blue light over the pump station at night.

## 9.3 PIET HEIN TUNNEL SERVICE BUILDING

**Address:** C. van Eesterenlaan 41
**Architect:** UN Studio
**Client:** Amsterdam Local Authority
**Year:** 1997

The 1900-metre long Piet Hein Tunnel, the longest in the Netherlands to date, has two tunnel corridors for cars and one for the tram to IJburg. The tunnel, which passes underneath the Amsterdam-Rhine Canal and the Spoorwegbassin, connects the A10 ring road with the eastern side of the city centre. The construction of the tunnel made it possible to exploit the spatial qualities of the eastern docklands with long strips of land surrounded by water. The tunnel consists of different tubing elements that are connected to one another by rubber profiles. These are pressed together so tightly by the water pressure that they make the tunnel waterproof. The concrete service buildings at the east and west entrances were designed by UN Studio, now one of the biggest firms of architects in the Netherlands with contracts all over the world. The buildings are almost entirely encased in sheets of perforated steel. Their shape is based on that of a box that has been distorted by torsion and twisting at the corners, resulting in a closed asymmetrical object that expresses the inaccessibility of this service building. The inside is illuminated at night.

## 9.4 STUDENT CONTAINERS

**Address:** Zuiderzeeweg 50-98
**Architect:** Fact Architects
**Client:** De Principaal
**Year:** 2010

Wedged between the IJburglaan tram line and the Transferium car park are 335 temporary dwellings for students. The complex consists of prefabricated units with the same properties as those to be found in regular housing and that satisfy future environmental criteria. The façade is uniformly clad with dark wooden elements. The facilities around the student accommodation were designed at the same time, such as the sports field, the post-boxes and the concrete benches. Eventually the complex will move to a definitive location.

## 9.5 EIBURGH SNACKS

**Address:** Zuiderzeeweg near 2

A converted marine container with a few appendages serves some of the best chips in Amsterdam, hand-cut from real potatoes. The stall occupies part of the service road of the Zuiderzeeweg – not exactly a beautiful view, but handy for cyclists to Waterland and for cars that can park on the terrace.

## 9.6 AMSTERDAM-RHINE CANAL

**Client:** Rijkswaterstaat
**Year:** 1952

The busy Amsterdam-Rhine Canal extends from the IJ to the Waal near Tiel and thereby connects the Amsterdam docks with the Ruhr region. It is a widened and lengthened version of the Merwede Canal that was constructed at the end of the nineteenth century. It was the engineer Anton Mussert, famous among other things for having been one of the founders of the Dutch National Socialist Movement (NSB), who thought of levelling the water between Amsterdam and the Lek in the 1930s by removing the locks to create a shorter and faster route. Later on the channel was widened and extended twice to accommodate container convoys with a depth of up to 3.3 metres.

## 9.7 NIEUWE DIEP

Year: 1651

In the past the Zuiderzee still posed a serious threat to the city and the countryside. The present-day Zeeburgerdijk and Diemerzeedijk were regularly exposed to high storm tides under which the dykes gave way. In 1422 the rising water right behind the dyke formed a small lake known as the Nieuwe Diep. The construction of the Merwede Canal, later the Amsterdam-Rhine Canal, cut it in two: the Benedendiep opposite the Flevopark and the Bovendiep opposite the Diemerzeedijk. In the first half of the twentieth century you could swim in the Zuiderzee natural swimming bath (admission two cents). Because of the polluted water, it was later replaced by the Flevobad. The development of IJburg has caused an increase of interest in the wetlands in the last few years. A plan has been drawn up for new recreational facilities that do not adversely affect the ecological values.

## 9.8 ZEEBURGERDIJK OOST

**Address:** Zeeburgerdijk 517-790, Flevoparkweg 2-114
**Architect:** Lafour en Wijk
**Client:** Woningbouwvereniging De Dageraad
**Year:** 2002

This complex beside the embankment of the Amsterdam bridge forms a transition to the Indische Buurt. The timber-clad blocks contain 155 owner-occupied and rented apartments. They are arranged tidily beside the dyke and more loosely beside the viaduct in a green setting. For a while there were temporary dwellings on and next to the historic Zeeburgerdijk. During the renewal of the area, the residents have called for the preservation of the mature trees and for environmentally aware and low-energy buildings. This has been facilitated by a government scheme of lower interest rates for green projects.

# 10. ENTREPOT WEST, BORNEO SPOREN-BURG AND KNSM ISLAND

By the late 1980s it had become clear that more than just cheap housing would have to be built in the city if it was to keep its middle class and stop them from migrating en masse to suburbs like Purmerend and Almere. Strips of exclusively rented council property were still being built in the 1980s beside the Cruquiusweg on the site of a former abattoir, but at the start of the following decade the Entrepot West project was the first experiment with private sector rented and owner-occupied properties with unusual architecture and urban planning that had a relation with the water. After this experiment had proved successful, the method was applied in other parts of the eastern area of the docks too, based on the principle of conservation of the structure of the harbour piers and basins. Another new feature was that no overarching plan was drawn up beforehand, but the KNSM island, Java island, Borneo Sporenburg and Oostelijke Handelskade were each successively developed on the basis of a master plan for each island.

The urban design for the former Borneo and Sporenburg marshalling yard, in use at the time for the transshipment of coal and ore, was heavily determined by the wish to implement many ground-level homes in a high density of 100 dwellings per hectare. Adriaan Geuze from West 8 Landscape Architects drew 'a sea of houses' with 'impacted meteorites'. Three superblocks with a total of 600 apartments were to be erected on unusual locations amid narrow streets with more than 1,500 low-rise housing blocks. Pacman and The Whale were implemented, but The Fountainhead has never got beyond the drawing board. Parking is mainly on residents' land and most of the dwellings are built back to back, though all with a roof terrace or patio and often with a separate room that can be used as a studio. The principle of 'blue for green' was applied to compensate the lack of green public space – the water belongs to everybody.

The KNSM island and the Java island arose from a breakwater, later a dyke, that was constructed at the end of the nineteenth century to protect the Oostelijke Handelskade. When the harbour activities expanded, the long dyke was widened to make room for the Royal Dutch Steamship Company (KNSM) and other shipping firms. After the shifting of the harbour westwards in the 1970s, urban nomads and artists appropriated the abandoned area. The KNSM island was the first part of the eastern docks to be redeveloped with 1,200 dwellings, though not without controversy. A plan with blocks at right angles to the water was defeated by a master plan drawn up by Jo Coenen: a wide city street in the centre and five monumental, robust superblocks facing the water. Memories of the dockland past are kept alive by the conservation of a number of old landmarks.

## 10.1 CRUQUIUS KWARTIER

*The Albeton company and its subsidiary MSA have been established on the Entrepothaven waterfront since 1977. The shiny silver silos are a striking landmark. The company supplies concrete mortar, anhydrite and other cement-related products from this central point. The raw materials are delivered by boat. Sand and gravel are also sold via the funnels.*

**Address:** Cruquiusweg 111
**Architect:** Dedato ontwerpers en architecten
**Client:** HVBM Vastgoed, PFC2 Vastgoed
**Year:** 2007

Like the buildings that Dedato designed in the Minervahaven, this business complex of four units takes on a robust industrial look through the use of rough concrete and glass. The units are twenty metres high, there are voids in the centre of each building, the interiors have a ceiling four metres high, and there are enormous glass façades in the side walls. The visible installations and the partly unfinished concrete elements on the inside wall give the impression of a studio. The rented units, which are of different sizes, can be linked vertically or horizontally, as the client chooses. The four penthouses on the topmost storey have a surface area of between 200 and 300 m2 and a panoramic view of the eastern docklands. Because housing is not allowed in this business park, they are designed to be used as offices.

*The Wine Terminal for the storage and transshipment of alcoholic beverages is at Cruquiusweg 67. It is no longer used for that purpose; the large industrial halls are occasionally used for parties and exhibitions.*

## 10.2 KOPGEBOUW

**Address:** Zeeburgerkade
**Architect:** Mulderblauw architecten
**Client:** VOF Kopgebouw, a collaboration of HBB Planontwikkeling and Fris Groep
**Year:** 2012

The customs sheds failed to obtain the status of a municipal monument; they were demolished, and the Kopgebouw is planned on the site. This project envisages a diversity of functions, including harbour facilities, a hotel, café, assembly and conference rooms, fitness amenities and business units. A large marina is also planned in the Entrepothaven with some 200 moorings.
The Zeeburg district organised a design competition for the location, which was won by Mulderblauw Architects. The design consists of a large volume with sloping façades in which various sections have been cut out. The hard natural stone outer wall contrasts with the softer inner wall of coloured sheets of glass. The entrances to the various functions are all grouped around the same patio. This is expected to produce a lively atmosphere on the slightly raised square. By setting the building at a slight angle to the quay, it refers to the 'meteorites' on Borneo and Sporenburg.

## 10.3 WAREHOUSES MAANDAG TO ZATERDAG

**Address:** Zeeburgerkade 152-826
**Architect:** Chris Smit
**Client:** Bouwfonds Nederlandse Gemeenten
**Year:** 1900 / 1991

The 300-metre long row of warehouses Maandag to Zaterdag [Monday to Saturday] was built at the turn of the century for the storage of transit goods which were exempt from import duty. It was an ideal location for that purpose: easily accessible by rail and water, and situated on the outskirts of the city. To prevent the goods from being smuggled into the country, high walls were built around the warehouses and a customs police station was established nearby (now: Boulevard Café). During the war the warehouses were used as storage depots for the Germans. With the shift of the docks from the east to the west, the warehouses lost their function, but not for long: the development of the eastern docklands as a residential district started with the renovation of this row of warehouses in the late 1980s. Although there was a lot of scepticism at first with regard to the feasibility of building housing in this area, the local authority eventually decided to go ahead.
The complex has been converted into 330 owner-occupied apartments, 110 of them with special subsidies. To allow daylight to enter, glass roofed inner streets have been made four storeys high which provide access to most of the apartments. Some of the dockland past of the buildings can still be seen in the protruding towers which used to house the hoisting installations and now accommodate the balconies.

## 10.4 WAREHOUSE ZONDAG

**Address:** Zeeburgerkade 30-148
**Architect:** Pieter Weeda
**Client:** Bouwfonds Nederlandse Gemeenten
**Year:** 1903 / 1992

Warehouse Zondag [Sunday] was built a few years after the series of warehouses named after the other days of the week and was specially designed for highly aromatic goods such as spices and tea. A new tablet in the wall overlooking the quay with a steaming teapot is a memorial of that past. The complex was converted into sixty owner-occupied apartments in the early 1990s. To ensure that daylight would penetrate the deep plot, it was decided to group the apartments around a large inner courtyard. The openings through which the bales of tea were hoisted inside in the past are now bays.

## 10.5 INTERNATIONAL INSTITUTE FOR SOCIAL HISTORY (IISG)

**Address:** Cruquiusweg 31
**Architect:** Wegener Sleeswijk, Atelier PRO
**Client:** Royal Netherlands Academy of Arts and Sciences
**Year:** 1961 / 1989

The former warehouse Willem II, which was built in 1961, now houses the Press Museum and the International Institute for Social History, the largest archive in the world for social history, containing the archives of such politicians as Troelstra and Den Uyl, but also documents of Karl Marx and Friedrich Engels, the Chinese student opposition and the squatter movement.
The reuse of the former warehouse for this function was only natural in this case. Willem II has a concrete construction and rests on columns 120 centimetres thick. The heavy load of more than 30,000 metres of archival material thus did not raise any problems at all for the construction.
Atelier PRO renovated the building, adding a number of openings to improve organisation and to allow light to enter, including a void on the side facing the water, as well as cladding the façade in insulation plaster.

## 10.6 ENTREPOTBRUG

**Address:** Entrepotbrug 55-218
**Architect:** Atelier PRO
**Client:** Muwi Vastgoed Rotterdam
**Year:** 1993

In the second half of the 1980s, after the rather monotonous housing on the site of the former abattoir had been completed, the Environmental Planning Department organised a multiple commission design competition for the Entrepot West planning zone. The winning plan for 600 homes – mainly council rented apartments but also some owner-occupied apartments, a phenomenon which was still novel at the time – included U-shaped semi-closed blocks, freestanding urban villas, and a five-storey apartment block which winds its serpentine way diagonally across the Entrepothaven. In spite of the uniform choice of materials – light grey masonry and plaster – the Entrepotbrug has a varied façade thanks to the alternation of balconies, galleries, rectangular and circular windows.
The size of the complex and the way in which its robust columns stand in the water make it the first in the development of the former docklands to engage with the scale of the surroundings, in which the harbour basins and railway are so characteristic.

## 10.7 PACMAN

*The name Pacman refers to one of the first computer games from 1980, in which the player manipulates a 'mouth', Pacman, that is supposed to eat all the coins in the field of play. That field is dangerous because of the spooks that can eliminate Pacman. The labyrinthine façade bears a resemblance to the field of this computer game.*

**Address:** R.J.H. Fortuynplein 2-214, R.J.H. Fortuynstraat 1-209
**Architect:** Koen van Velsen
**Client:** SFB BPF Bouw
**Year:** 1998

The Pacman building, which accommodates 207 apartments, is one of the three superblocks or 'meteorites' on Borneo Sporenburg which give the suburban area a metropolitan allure. The building breaks up the pattern of long parallel streets on the island. It has been deliberately placed at an angle in the continuation of the Oranjesluizen, even though they are a long way away when you are on the spot.
The architect's design emphasises the building as a utility and expresses this in its appearance. The complex makes a large and ponderous impression because of the use of dark brick, steel and wood. At the same time, however, the façade is very varied with different types of apartment, shops and business units.
A wooden 'curtain' has been adopted for the façade, behind which the different functions remain in view. It is noteworthy that the three-level car park is clearly visible. The word 'Borneo' has been stamped into the grid on the Borneokade side.

## 10.8 DE OCEAAN

**Address:** R.J.H. Fortuynplein 11-29
**Architect:** CASA architecten
**Client:** Stoomvaartmaatschappij De Oceaan / De Principaal
**Year:** 1951 / 1999

The only tangible memory of the dockland past of Borneo Sporenburg is the building called De Oceaan [The Ocean]. It was built as a canteen and office building for the steamshipping company of the same name. The sheds that stood around it have been demolished. It has been converted into three owner-occupied apartments, five council rented apartments with studios, and a restaurant. A lot of attention has been paid to restoring the original style of the façades. The rusted steel frames with stool profiles have been replaced by aluminium frames with thermal separation. To avoid visible duct silencers and ventilation grills in the façade, balanced ventilation with heat recovery was adopted.

## 10.9 FREE BUILDING PLOTS

**Address:** Scheepstimmermanstraat
**Architect:** different architects
**Client:** private
**Year:** 1999

One of the main architectural attractions of recent Amsterdam architecture is the row of homes in the Scheepstimmermanstraat. Though that was not the prior intention, this section of the street is a sampler of the architectural taste of the late twentieth century. Prompted by the national policy of encouraging individual building initiatives, the local authority conducted an experiment on Borneo by issuing sixty plots of building land to private builders. After registration, private individuals who were selected by lot could build their dream home here. The future residents and their architects – sometimes experienced, sometimes not – were coached in workshops to direct this unique building project in the city through the right channels.
There was nevertheless strict supervision by Adriaan Geuze, who was responsible for the master plan of the area, to ensure some measure of consistency in the buildings.
The limiting conditions included a minimal ground floor height of 3.5 metres, the same condition that applies to all of the low-rise buildings on Borneo Sporenburg. The façades must combine to form a closed street wall. Brick, untreated wood and little or no colour were prescribed, but in the course of the building process other façade materials were eventually accepted.
As for parking, the idea was that it would be done on the owner's own land, which led to ingenious solutions.

The design and interior of most of the houses have been made to measure. From both the street side and the water side – there is a view from the bridge to and from the Stokerkade – it is easy to see that each of the designs is unique and that the whole is easy to place in a particular period.

## 10.10 BRIDGES OVER SPOORWEGBASSIN

*If you want to stay in one of the 'home-made' homes, you can do so at Bottelierplein 2, where the architect has opened one of the DIY plots, a room and a suite entirely in the style of modern architecture of the surroundings, as a B&B.*

**Architect:** West 8 urban design and landscape architecture
**Client:** Gemeentelijk Grondbedrijf Amsterdam
**Year:** 2001
The firm that drew up the master plan for Borneo Sporenburg also designed two striking red bridges to connect Borneo and Sporenburg. The westernmost bridge is low and is suitable for cyclists and wheelchair users. The eastern pedestrian bridge rises in an arch to a height of twelve metres. The top offers a view of the roof landscape of the low-rise housing with the numerous patios. Pleasure boats can pass beneath the bridge and children use the spectacular height in the summer as a diving board to plunge into the water.
Both bridges are made of steel T-profiles with a red industrial paint that lights up at night. The profiles combine to form a membrane that gives the bridges their sculptural form. The deck and railing are of untreated wood. The lighting consists of cast aluminium fittings in the form of gull's heads.

## 10.11 KEESJE BRIJDE PLANTSOEN

*In his scruffy threadbare clothes*
*With nothing to eat*
*Little Amsterdam kid*
*Little rascal of the street*

This is a verse from the poem next to the white cross, a monument to Keesje Brijde that stands on the Panamakade. It was written by J. Schagen while the war was still in progress. It refers to the sad story of the twelve-year-old Keesje, one of a family of thirteen children. During the Hunger Winter of 1944, he and other children searched the shunting yard for coal that had fallen from the trains, sometimes three times a day. Everyone at home was suffering from the cold and there was nothing to eat. The shunting yard was patrolled and was forbidden territory. When the children were caught, they were shut up in a special wagon. A German security guard threatened: 'If I catch you again, I'll shoot you dead!'. He was true to his word. Keesje was shot in the neck and died in hospital soon afterwards. The space that has been left as a diagonal strip between the three slat-shaped apartment blocks of Sporenburg is the only greenery on Borneo Sporenburg.

**Year:** 1944 / 2000

## 10.12 FRAGMENT OF A LIVING ROOM REDUCED TO 88%

**Address:** P.E. Tegelbergplein
**Artist:** Mark Manders
**Client:** Amsterdam Fund for the Arts
**Year:** 2001

A work of art by Mark Manders stands on the quiet cobbled square at the end of Sporenburg. It represents a fragment of a living room. There are two figures on a table who at first sight seem identical, but closer inspection shows that they are two successive moments of the same figure, with a minuscule difference in facial expression and posture.

## 10.13 SINGLE-FAMILY HOMES

*There are far more children in the eastern docklands than had originally been anticipated. Many residents look for ways of extending their home. In the last few years many storage facilities and patios have been converted into extra rooms. Since it often happened that several owners worked with the same architect, the appearance of the façade has remained fairly uniform.*

**Address:** Ertskade 1-103
**Architect:** Claus en Kaan Architecten (85-103), Köther en Salman (61-83), Ruth Visser (45-59), Neutelings Riedijk Architecten (1-43)
**Client:** Ontwikkelingsmaatschappij New Deal
**Year:** 1998

Various firms of architects have worked on the assignment to build single-family dwellings on Borneo Sporenburg with a very high density of 100 per hectare. Some built projects on several plots, often as variations on the same theme. How the concept of back-to-back patio homes with a width of 4.2 metres on a long and narrow building plot has been interpreted and which variations are possible within the fixed framework of guidelines is clear from this row of homes, which were the first to be built on the Ertskade. Homes designed by four different firms of architects stand side by side in the same way as the rest of the low-rise buildings: respect for the building line, clear choice of materials, predominantly reddish-brown brick, much parking on the occupant's own land, and a closed outdoor space that turns its back on the street.

## 10.14 THE FOUNTAINHEAD

**Address:** Ertskade
**Architect:** KCAP Architects & Planners
**Client:** Fountainhead Enterprise bv (De Key, Eigen Haard)
**Year:** 2014

The Fountainhead designed by KCAP Architects & Planners for the quay of the Ertskade was intended to be the third meteorite, following the original urban design plan, with one foot in the water and one on land. With an envelope of more than 60 x 60 x 60 metres, the project with three tower blocks and twenty floors containing 237 apartments, a primary school, business units and parking facilities may be as high as the Skydome and the IJtoren near the Verbindingsdam. Although the building permit has been issued and is irrevocable, it is still not clear when the building will go up in view of the economic crisis. The temporary function of a football field – popular with the youngsters in the neighbourhood – will be maintained for the time being.

## 10.15 THE WHALE

**Address:** Baron G.A. Tindalstraat 2-240, Baron G.A. Tindalplein 1-149
**Architect:** de Architekten Cie. (Frits van Dongen)
**Client:** Ontwikkelingsmaatschappij New Deal
**Year:** 2001

The Whale, one of the three meteorites of Borneo Sporenburg, owes its name to the image it conjures up of a beached whale because of its enormous size, the unusual folded form, and the uniform silver façade material. The ends of the building have been raised to create a gradual transition from the public space to the closed block and to ensure that the water of the harbour can be seen from the inner courtyard. The sloping roof lines are based on studies of sunlight and allow optimal penetration of light. There are more than two hundred apartments in The Whale. The access system of the building is a variant of the regular gallery: the apartments grouped around the courtyard are accessed at every other floor by galleries which are interconnected by stairs.

## 10.16 VERBINDINGSDAM

**Architect:** Hans van Heeswijk architecten
**Client:** Dienst IVV
**Year:** 1997

The name Verbindingsdam [connecting dam] goes back to when the link between the KNSM island and the Java island was still a dam with a goods train line that connected the islands with the mainland. The old bridge had to be replaced to increase the traffic capacity and to make the bridge suitable for trams. The oblique angle of the dam and bridge in relation to the riverbanks is a result of its previous use: the trains that travelled from Sporenburg to the Java island were unable to negotiate a sharp bend. The possibility of straightening the connection from the Panamalaan was considered to facilitate the flow of traffic, but was turned down in the face of local protest. The bridge, designed by Hans van Heeswijk, is very wide in relation to the span. That would have given it a relatively heavy appearance. That is why the surface of the bridge was divided into three separate, parallel sections to allow light to enter in between. The construction of the bridge is located in these voids and consists of two pairs of steel arches supported by seven transverse beams.

## 10.17 MIEN RUYSPLANTSOEN

**Address:** KNSM-laan
**Architect:** Mien Ruys
**Client:** KNSM
**Year:** 1956 / 1995

The landscape architect Mien Ruys designed an elongated park on the south side of the peninsula for the KNSM in the 1950s. It was a park where personnel and passengers who were saying farewell could take a stroll. The design is characterised by a diagonal play of lines that broke up the elongated shapes of the buildings, and is typical of Ruys' work of the period. She often worked with architects from the New Building movement at the time and tried to find an answer to the rectangular plots that were so common in the architecture of the postwar reconstruction period. Her nickname then was Diagonal Mien.

With the development of the KNSM island in the 1990s, only a small part of the park was left. Mien Ruys, who had reached the age of 89 by then, was invited by the supervisor to come up with a new design. Only the diagonal pond could be preserved, and that determined the line of the new design. A few of the large trees from the original design could also be incorporated in the new one. Diagonal pedestrian routes connect roads and paths logically with one another. The park is connected with the enclosed garden of the Piraeus block by means of an opening with a colonnade.

## 10.18 PIRAEUS

**Address:** KNSM-laan 204-610, Levantkade 51-149, Piraeusplein 2-32, 1-75
**Architect:** Hans Kollhoff with Christian Rapp
**Client:** De Doelen
**Year:** 1994

The Piraeus block by the Berlin architect Hans Kollhoff is the most eye-catching of all the projects on the KNSM island. The sculptural form clad with dark-brown brick towers above the waterfront. This was the first building to be completed on the KNSM island and had a strong influence on the architectural debate on large-scale housing at the time.
More than 300 apartments have been distributed among the four to eight storeys. Most of them are rented council flats, while a couple of large patio apartments have been placed under the roof.
Because the former KNSM administration and mustering building had been rescued thanks to the dedication of the squatters, the Piraeus has been folded inwards around the old building, as it were. The tips enclose two inner courtyards. This unusual shape serves to temper the large dimensions.
The south side is characterised by the steel frames that have been placed between the brickwork without any recessing, giving the façade a flat and sober look. The folding windows can be completely opened so that the verandah can be used both as a winter garden and as a balcony.
With a large terrace on the quayside overlooking the harbour, Café Kanis & Meiland for coffee, drinks and snacks for old and young has been established on the ground floor from the first. It is a place for locals and visitors to hang out. The name of this café does not refer to the past – it plays on the name KNSM island as pronounced in Dutch.

## 10.19 KNSM CANTEEN

**Address:** Levantplein 1-15
**Architect:** CASA architecten
**Client:** Stichting Edelweis
**Year:** 1962 / 1991

The former canteen building, which rests on columns, was built for the KNSM dockers. Soon after it fell into disuse in the 1980s it was squatted by artists. In consultation with the local authority, the building changed hands for the symbolic price of one guilder, and agreement was reached on the renovation, which left the interiors of the studio apartments as the occupants had arranged them intact. However, the building application was turned down because the building was only accessible on one side and therefore failed to comply with fire safety regulations. The entire initiative was on the point of being dropped when at the last moment ship's staircases found on a demolition site happened to become available and provided each apartment with its own access. The artists were not allowed to sell their homes for ten years. By now a number of the very spacious apartments have been put on the market and sold for astronomical sums.

## 10.20 BARCELONAPLEIN

**Address:** Levantkade 169-263, Barcelonaplein 1-177, 2-180, KNSM-laan 612-754
**Architect:** Bruno Albert
**Client:** Het Oosten
**Year:** 1993

This project by the Belgian architect Bruno Albert has a clear Neo-Classical look about it. Two seven-storey semicircles encircle a public square. Two five-storey U-shaped sections meet the convex sides of the semicircles, with which they enclose two private inner courtyards. A total of 321 apartments of various types have been distributed over the whole block. They are almost all rented council flats, ranging from one-room to six-room apartments, group apartments, and apartments for wheelchair users. The small semicircular balconies in front of all the windows overlooking the square and the layered alternation of dark and white brick deliberately bring about a distortion of scale. On the level of the square the palazzo seems at first sight to be very spacious, but the height of the balcony fencing betrays the low ceilings of the council apartments. In this respect the complex recalls the architecture of the Barcelona architect Ricardo Bofill, who made a name for himself with his Neo-Classical council flat complexes in the suburbs of Paris at the beginning of the 1980s. The name of the square is an allusion to the shipping line that the KNSM ran to the Catalonian capital.

## 10.21 FENCE

**Address:** Barcelonaplein
**Artist:** Narcisse Tordoir
**Client:** Werkgroep Kunst Oostelijk Havengebied
**Year:** 1993

The Belgian artist Narcisse Tordoir has placed a work of art at the southern entrance to the circular Barcelonaplein. It has the form of a monumental fence that follows the curve of the building. Tordoir's work combines small, usually painted little panels to form ensembles. It is subdivided into squares of 3.3 by 3.3 metres; the steel contours in each square can be read as scenes from a crudely drawn comic strip. The rectangular grid, the artist states, is at the same time a reaction to the rhythm of the architecture of Bruno Albert.

## 10.22 EMERALD EMPIRE

**Address:** Venetiëhof 1-224
**Architect:** Jo Coenen & Co Architekten
**Client:** Verwelius / Eurowoningen
**Year:** 1996 / 1998

While Jo Coenen drew up the master plan for the KNSM island and supervised the architecture, he himself designed a superblock on the most striking location at the eastern tip of the island as a monumental conclusion to the KNSM-laan. The contrast between the spaciousness of the surroundings and use of inner courtyards to create a sense of being closed, which runs through the whole of the master plan, finds very literal expression here in this cylindrical block with ground plans that fan out. The 224 apartments distributed over eight storeys and available to owner occupiers are almost all of the same type. They all have deeply framed balconies in a varied rhythm to give the façade a lot of expression. Access to the apartments from the protected inner courtyard is via a gallery. Jo Coenen designed seven semi-detached homes and, on a lower level, thirteen riverside homes 'like a pearl necklace' around the Emerald Empire. In fact this row of villas with private ground for parking is in complete contrast to the master plan, which is based on medium-height superblocks. The villas are designed in a rectangular functionalist style and are plastered in light grey. Access to the riverside homes is on the street side. They have a narrow terrace directly beside the water.

## 10.23 SOCRATES, PERICLES, ARCHIMEDES AND DIOGENES

**Address:** KNSM-laan 527-891
**Architect:** Frank and Paul Wintermans
**Client:** Eurowoningen
**Year:** 1994

The tricky part about designing on this shallow and elongated plot was that the best view is to the north, while the sun is in the south. This is reflected in the external appearance of the four apartment blocks in a flat façade facing the windy Surinamekade, three of them in light concrete.
The horizontally articulated red brick façade on the KNSM-laan side shows more differentiation, with internal balconies, a recessed top floor with roof terraces, and overhanging balconies on the side blocks.

## 10.24 SKYDOME

**Address:** KNSM-laan 327-525
**Architect:** Wiel Arets Architects
**Client:** Wilma Bouw
**Year:** 1996

The sixty-metre Skydome is one of the tallest blocks of apartments in Amsterdam. The façade consists of dark-grey concrete elements with a relief, giving it the appearance of natural stone. The building has a rather monotonous look because of the regular distribution of the windows and balconies and the fact that only one colour has been used. It functions as a landmark for the island when seen from a distance and it is not for nothing that it has earned the nickname The Black Madonna.
The 100 owner occupied three-room and four-room apartments are distributed over twenty-one floors. The apartments on the north side have a side balcony so that all of the residents can enjoy the sun.

## 10.25 LOODS 6 AND KOMPASZAAL

**Addres:** KNSM-laan 311
**Architect:** Jan Tienhoven / Villanova
**Client:** KNSM / Stichting Kunstwerk Loods 6
**Year:** 1900 / 1956 / 1997

Loods 6, which is now a business complex with interior and furniture shops in the plinth, was built at the beginning of 1900 by the Royal Dutch Steamship Company (KNSM) as a transshipment and customs shed. In the mid-1950s the shipping architect Jan Tienhoven was commissioned to turn part of the building into a passenger terminal with the baggage hall on the ground floor. The most striking feature is the authentic first-floor Kompaszaal [Compass Hall] on the east side with a wide balcony overlooking the IJ. Now it is a café-restaurant, but it was used at the time as the departure hall for first-class passengers with the KNSM. A number of artists worked on the decoration of the hall and entrance. The interior contains a mural by Cuno van den Steene and a glass wall by Lex Horn. There are two mosaics by Dick ten Hoedt, representing 'The Leave-taking' and 'The Family', in the vestibule on the ground floor.

## 10.26 KOMPASEILAND

Kompaseiland [Compass island] is a small patch of green land in the middle of the IJ opposite Loods 6. It was constructed a long time ago for shipping, as a calibration point to set the compass before setting out on a long voyage. Now, however, this patch of dry land has triggered a variety of plans, from an extra mooring place for inland craft to – in an enlarged version – a green recreational area for the residents of the eastern docklands. There are also ideas to use it as a support point for a bridge over the IJ. Nothing is happening for the time being, and the compass plant is still free to proliferate here. This harbour plant is not named after the island, but because the tips of the leaves point in a North-South direction in the sun. The plant probably comes from the Orient and may have been brought here by ships from remote regions.

## 10.27 AMPHITRITE AND TRITON

**Address:** KNSM-laan, central reservation
**Artist:** Albert Termote
**Client:** Employees of the KNSM
**Year:** 1956 / 2009

There is a striking sculptural group in a fountain in the green central reservation at the beginning of the KNSM-laan: Amphitrite, wife of the god of the sea Poseidon, sits waving on the back of a mythological creature that looks like a rearing horse whose body ends in that of a fish. Amphitrite is accompanied by her son Triton, half-human and half-fish, who is blowing a shell. The group also includes a dolphin and part of an anchor.
The work was made by the Dutch-Flemish sculptor Albert Termote, who is mainly known for his equestrian statues. It was a present from the employees of the KNSM to celebrate the hundredth anniversary of the firm. When the KNSM closed down here, the sculptural group was transferred to the Amsterdam local authority and was 'lost' for a time. After an unsuitable temporary location in the Oosterdok, this monument of the past is now back on its original location.

## 10.28 HOOGWERF AND HOOGKADE

**Address:** Azartplein 2-16, KNSM-laan 2-98, Bogortuin 3-255
**Architect:** Diener & Diener Architekten
**Client:** Amstelland Vastgoed
**Year:** 2001

The two large monotonous apartment blocks — one elongated, the other square — in red-brown brick with identical windows, that stand on either side of the Verbindingsdam, form the transition from the KNSM island to the Java island. The idea for a transitional block of this kind was already fixed at an early stage of the planning. In 1995 the local authority commissioned a couple of big firms of architects with an international reputation to carry out a multiple investigation of the possibilities, and the design by the Swiss firm Diener & Diener was the successful one.
The Hoogkade block on the side of the Java island is an elongated block of 127 apartments. It stands partly in the water on newly raised ground in the angle between the island and the dam. There is a large parking facility in the basement that also caters for the residents of the other block. The entrance is behind a long wall to protect it from the cold north side adjoining the Azartplein.
The Hoogwerf block has 45 apartments and business units. It borders on the Mien Ruysplantsoen. An unusual feature of the ground plans of Hoogwerf is that the rooms, usually three, are of the same size. This means that the apartment can be divided up in a variety of ways, for example for duo housing, or a combination of private and work space.

*Plans for bridges over the IJ are nothing new. The Amsterdam sub-contractor Galman made no less than 36 designs for such a bridge between 1851 and 1886 because of irritation at the hold-ups on the water. None of them was implemented because of the limited economic significance of North Holland and the fear of sedimentation around the columns. It was not until after the Second World War that permanent links from bank to bank were created in the form of tunnels and of the Schellingwouderbrug on the east side of the city. All the same, speculations about a permanent bridge over the IJ do pop up now and then. For instance, there are ideas for extending the Jan Schaeferbrug over the IJ into the Hamerstraat district. A study is also being carried out on a bridge between the Houthavens and the NDSM wharf. It is a difficult assignment, because the IJ carries heavy traffic and there is little room for a bridge landing on the banks.*

# 11. JAVA ISLAND AND PIET HEINKADE

The opening of the North Sea Canal in 1876 immediately put the eastern docklands and the Oostelijke Handelskade on the wrong side of the city. Because of the drop in the number of shipping lines as a result of air transportation and because commodities were no longer stored in warehouses but in containers, the eastern docklands only operated at full steam for a relatively brief period. In the 1970s the harbour activities began to move westwards and after a period of vacancy and all kinds of forms of temporary use, the area has been redeveloped over the last fifteen years to become a mixed residential, work and recreation district.
The Java island was tackled after the KNSM island. The architect and urban designer Sjoerd Soeters drew up the master plan and divided the elongated peninsula into five blocks. Fourteen different architects each designed a housing block – each with the same width of 27 metres and a fixed dimension of 5.4 metres – that could be repeated in different combinations on several plots. This resulted in varied façades in terms of the choice of materials and colours. The urban blocks with intimate but public courtyards are separated by four canals lined with smaller individual dwellings.
Motorised through traffic is led through the slightly curving north side facing the IJ. The buildings are higher on that side than on the sunny south side overlooking the IJhaven, where the quay is only accessible to residents. Cyclists cross the island via the route through the courtyards where the wind is less. Most parking on the whole island is underground.
The urban development plan for the Piet Heinkade, the former Oostelijke Handelskade that runs parallel to the railway track, was drawn up by Hans van der Made from the Environmental Planning Department.
It is based on the model of a train, with old and new warehouses as the wagons and the Muziekgebouw aan 't IJ as the locomotive at the head of the train. The limiting conditions for the architects were formulated in such a way that it should not be possible to tell from the façade whether the buildings accommodated apartments or offices. There is a large mixture of functions here, with apartments in every price category, cultural functions, offices, shops and catering.

## 11.1 HET EINDE VAN DE WERELD

*Unlike the KNSM island, hardly any of the original buildings have been preserved on the Java island. The only one left is the Samenwerkende Havenbedrijven building from 1918 on what is now Azartplein 1-47. Squatters and the De Doelen housing corporation have elaborated a plan to turn it into housing units (some with studio) and business units.*

**Address:** Javakade 61

You can eat a healthy meal every Wednesday and Friday on board the *Quo Vadis*. This former squatters' restaurant, Het Einde van de Wereld [The End of the World], run by volunteers started in 1984 in the former office building of the Cornelder shipping company on the Sumatrakade. Sometimes you have to queue up outside on the desolate quayside before you can draw up to the long tables. An attempt was made to preserve the building as one of the few remnants of the past of the Java island, but when furnace oil was found in the ground it proved impossible to carry out cleaning up operations without demolition. The restaurant has been continued in the canal boat moored to the quayside.

## 11.2 BRIDGES

**Architect:** Paul Wintermans, G. Rombouts, M. Droste
**Client:** Gemeentelijk Grondbedrijf Amsterdam
**Year:** 2000

The whimsical and amusing black ironwork bridges over the canals for pedestrians and cyclists are all different. They were designed by the Belgian artistic duo Rombouts-Droste. They devised an alphabet of their own consisting of words with an emotional association that they incorporated in the bridge, although it is not really possible for the unsuspecting visitor to translate them. The bridge covered with curved arches is a reference to the word 'idea', and the steep bridge with steps represents the word 'light'. The bridges clad in brick for motorised traffic on the north side along the Sumatrakade were designed by Paul Wintermans in a much more sober style.

## 11.3 SOETERS APARTMENT BLOCKS

**Adress:** Sumatrakade 195-237, 285-325, 1157-1191, Javakade 516-542, 580-618 en 700-728
**Architect:** Sjoerd Soeters
**Client:** BPF Bouw
**Year:** 1997

The most colourful blocks on the Java island were designed by Sjoerd Soeters, author of the master plan and supervisor. The flat façades on the Sumatrakade catch the eye with their green, pink, yellow, purple, orange, blue, turquoise and red corrugated apron walls.
On the Javakade the blocks are different in character: a steel grid affords a view of the façade in white plastic panels. Large entrances clad with red sheeting give access to and a view of the inner courtyards, or even from one side of the island to the other. Soeters himself designed another block of apartments on the Java island, on the corner of the Sumatrakade and the Lamonggracht, but that is relatively inconspicuously finished with prefab concrete panels clad with red-brown tiles.

## 11.4 CRUZ Y ORTIZ APARTMENT BLOCKS

The firm of the Spanish architects Antonio Cruz and Antonio Ortiz is responsible for the renovation and extension of the Rijksmuseum in Amsterdam, but they have worked in Amsterdam before. On the Java island they designed two free-standing buildings with one-family homes on the central area and six blocks with different types of apartment on the waterfronts, distributed among the five courtyards into which the island has been divided.
The basic design for all the blocks consists of prefab façade elements of yellow-orange brick with a minimal width of joint, interrupted by windows with cream-coloured wooden panels on either side. The window openings and loggias are cut out of the façade as continuous horizontal strips. The blocks designed by the Spanish duo are fairly sober in appearance by comparison with the multi-coloured buildings of the rest of the Java island.

**Address:** Sumatrakade 13-51, 241-279, 853-891, 1249-1293, Imogirituin 1-55, Javakade 364-398, 544-578, 664-698
**Architect:** Cruz y Ortiz
**Client:** SFB, BPF Bouw
**Year:** 1997

## 11.5 JAVA CANAL HOUSES

**Address:** Lamonggracht 3-17, 6-20, Brantasgracht 7-21, 2-16
**Architect:** John Bosch, Dana Ponec, Architectenbureau Marlies Rohmer, Architectenbureau Art Zaaijer, Jos van Eldonk, C. Heuff, René van Zuuk Architekten, M. De Maeseneer, G. Kruunenberg
**Client:** SFB, BPF Bouw
**Year:** 1998–2000

Various young architects, and in some cases the younger partners of large firms of architects, were invited to design the canal houses beside the four newly created canals. Each of them designed a house that is repeated several times in a different sequence each time. As a result, no canal is exactly the same as another. The width of the building plot is only 4.5 metres, but within that limitation the architects were free to use their imagination.

The canalside buildings appeared in two stages. The first batch, beside the Brantasgracht and Lamong-gracht, is more extravagant in design than the second batch, beside the Majanggracht and the Seranggracht, where the façades are somewhat stricter and have less protruding elements. Eye-catchers from the first batch are the verandahs framed with planks and set at an angle by Dana Ponec, the sloping zinc façade clad with slate by Jos van Eldonk, and the wide concrete frames of the windows in the houses designed by Marlies Rohmer. The façades by Art Zaaijer are high tech with glass, aluminium and iron. The outstanding designs from the second batch are the severe details of the windows by Bjarne Masten-broek, ROW Architectuur and Dick van Gameren. Onix designed façades with wide black planks on the level of the topmost storeys which refer to the wooden façades of houses in the polders of North Holland. Marx & Steketee used copper and zinc

**Address:** Seranggracht 1-15, 4-18, Majanggracht 3-18,
**Architect:** Babet Galis, Bjarne Mastenbroek, Dick van Gameren, D. de Meijer, R. Onsia, W.H. Schenk, ROW Architectuur, Marx & Steketee architecten, Onix Architekten
**Client:** Moes Bouwbedrijf
**Year:** 2000

as façade cladding to reinforce the diversity in the façades of the canal even more.
There is no comparison with the canals in the historic city centre, because some of the houses there were built centuries before others. But the variegated whole of the buildings alongside the canals of the Java island gives a good impression of the Postmodern architectural idiom of the late 1990s.

## 11.6 AMICITIA, CONCORDIA, HOLLANDIA, OLYMPIA, BATAVIA AND HISPANIA

**Address:** Sumatrakade 1297-1341, 1391-1433, 1483-1537, Tosaristraat 5-31
**Architect:** Karelse van der Meer Architecten, Cees Nagelkerke, baneke van der hoeven architecten
**Client:** Moes Bouwbedrijf
**Year:** 1997

The idea of the master plan was for the Java island to evoke an image reminiscent of the canals in the historic centre of Amsterdam: each building resembles its neighbours in terms of size, details and colour, but if you look closely you can see that the details are different. Karelse van der Meer Architecten tackled their assignment in the same spirit. They gave the four nine-storey blocks a character of their own through differences in orientation, use of colour, and the design of the entrances.
The Batavia and Hispania blocks in the same row and commissioned by the same client also have nine storeys. Batavia was designed by Cees Nagelkerke, Hispania by baneke van der hoeven architekten. Nagelkerke's façade emphasises the vertical dimension by making the brick window piers stand out sharply between the large window strips, alternating with light-beige sheeting. Baneke van der hoeven designed a large window strip that protrudes slightly from the façade. The topmost storeys consist of apartments with a glass skylight over two floors plus a roof terrace.

## 11.7 PRIMARY SCHOOL PLUS

*During the development of the Java island, this western tip was deliberately left empty. There were plenty of wild plans, but it was decided to leave this spectacular location for a while until an appropriate metropolitan function should arrive. A special commission has been set up, known as the Kloos commission after the chairman Maarten Kloos from the Architecture Centre Amsterdam. It considers the plans submitted once a year and advises the city administration, but so far its recommendations have always been negative. In the meantime the empty site is used as a site for festivals, a skating alley, and a parking place for buses.*

**Address:** Tosaristraat 30
**Architect:** NAT architecten
**Client:** Amsterdam Development Corporation (OGA)
**Year:** 2010

Sometimes a building can go up very quickly, like this temporary one at the tip of the Java island that houses a primary school plus crèche, afterschool facility, gym, language lab, library and domestic science centre. Exactly one year intervened between the first sketch by NAT architecten and the completion. The actual building process lasted nineteen weeks. The interior, that was designed by the same architects, was completed in four weeks with a prefab building system. The façade is clad with a semi-transparent sheeting with a mother-of-pearl sheen which changes colour depending on from which angle you view it. The building permit is for five years. The building can be dismantled and reassembled on a different site.

## 11.8 MARINER ON THE LOOKOUT

**Address:** Kop Javaeiland
**Artist:** Pieter Starreveld
**Client:** Stoomvaart Maatschappij Nederland
**Year:** 1950

At the very tip of the Java island stands the monument *Mariner on the Lookout*, also known as Joop Hoorn after a boatswain who lived on the Javakade. The labrador granite statue was done in 1950 by Pieter Starreveld, a Dutch sculptor who made various memorial monuments after the Second World War. It symbolises the mariner who, dressed in oilskins and sou'wester with his hand above his eyes, peers in the direction of the North Sea Canal as he awaits the arrival of seafarers. It is a memorial to the victims of the Stoomvaart Maatschappij Nederlands, later the Koninklijke Lloyd, which was established on the Java island from 1910 to 1968.

## 11.9 IJTOREN

**Address:** Veemkade 1288-1312, Oostelijke Handelskade 1065-1213
**Architect:** Neutelings Riedijk Architects
**Client:** Blauwhoed
**Year:** 1998

This 60-metre-high apartment tower block on the corner of the Verbindingsdam and the Piet Heinkade is an important landmark in the eastern docklands. Bites have been taken out of the façade at various points so that every floor is different. In line with the trend of the late 1990s, there are twenty different types of owner-occupied apartment in a total of 68. There is a car park on the first floor. The façades are clad with broad vertical elements made of reinforced fibre plate, which are accentuated by aluminium connection profiles. The choice of a different material gives extra emphasis to the recessed parts of the façade. It is striking that the windows are not placed directly beneath one another, but are staggered.

## 11.10 BRAZILIË SHOPPING CENTRE

**Address:** Veemkade 1224-1286, Oostelijke Handelskade 1001-1063
**Architect:** Neutelings Riedijk Architects
**Client:** Blauwhoed Vastgoed
**Year:** 1998

At first sight the Brazilië shopping centre seems to be a new construction, but the complex consists of an iron skeleton and the roof trusses of the original Koninklijke Hollandse Lloyd Brazil coffee and cocoa warehouse dating from 1915. The warehouse was razed to the ground and the material reused as the basis for this new shopping centre slightly west of the original site.

## 11.11 ODESSA AND LIZBOA

**Addres:** Cruquiusweg 31
**Architect:** Wegener Sleeswijk, Atelier PRO
**Client:** Royal Netherlands Academy of Arts and Sciences
**Year:** 1961 / 1989

Moored near the shopping centre is a replica of a Russian merchant vessel, the *Odessa*, from and named after the Ukrainian port of the same name. It has been thoroughly renovated and is used as a café-restaurant. Nearby is *Lizboa*, now a party ship as well, with a terrace on the deck. This ship was launched in 1894 under the name *Rhein* and has had many functions from steam tug on the German rivers to training ship for bargees' children and base for a sailing school. The Drijfgoed company renovated it in 1999 and gave it the new name *Lizboa*.

## 11.12 LLOYD COFFEE HOUSE AMSTERDAM

**Address:** Oostelijke Handelskade 44
**Architect:** Evert Breeman / CASA architecten
**Client:** Woningstichting Zomers Buiten
**Year:** 1917 / 2003

The Koninklijke Hollandsche Lloyd coffee house was built in 1917 by the same architect who designed the Lloyd Hotel. The front room was the decorous domain of the higher-ranking personnel, while the dockhands and day labourers ate their sandwiches and pea soup in the back room. Unemployed labourers also came here to apply for work and could drink a cup of coffee there for ten cents. The coffee house disappeared when the company did. After the war the premises housed a grocer's shop and a souvenir wholesaler. Since 2003 it has regained its original function, but without the division between front and back rooms. It is used not only as a café-restaurant but also as a meeting place and assembly room for the neighbourhood.

## 11.13 LLOYD HOTEL

**Address:** Oostelijke Handelskade 34
**Architect:** Evert Breeman / MVRDV
**Client:** Woonstichting De Key
**Year:** 1918 / 2004

Few buildings on the banks of the IJ have such a turbulent history behind them as the Lloyd Hotel, now one of the cultural hot spots of the city. As part of a complex including offices, accommodation for personnel and a delousing building, it was taken into use in 1921 as a hotel for migrants: Jewish refugees and peasants from Eastern Europe spent the night here waiting for the Koninklijke Lloyd ships that sailed for South America once every three weeks. Because they were not allowed to leave the premises during that period, the building could provide everything they needed: shops, a small hospital, restaurants, and even a kosher kitchen.

After the Lloyd shipping company went into liquidation in 1935 – one of the reasons for the bankruptcy was the high expense of building this hotel – the building passed into the hands of the local authority.

Because of its isolated position at the time, it was used as a prison for resistance fighters during World War Two, and later as a detention centre and remand home until 1989. When the building no longer met the criteria of the prison service, it was used by artists as a studio. Although the surroundings were renovated on a large scale, the building declined more and more. A round of new plans for it began in 1997, which resulted in its renovation as a hotel with a catering function and a so-called Cultural Embassy.

The MVRDV firm of architects had to abide by strict regulations because by now the Lloyd Hotel had been put on the list of preserved national historic monuments. It retained its classical, dark exterior with decorative masonry in a mixed style of Art Déco and Dutch Renaissance elements. But inside there have been major changes. The introduction of a large, central void brought in much more light. An unusual feature is that each of the 116 hotel rooms is different, not only in comfort but also in design. Different designers, including the artist Joep van Lieshout, devised the design of each room. There are one-star rooms with a shared shower in the corridor, and highly individualised five-star suites: a room with an eight-person bed, a very high room with a grand piano to suit a travelling musician, a room with an open bathroom, or an entirely wood-panelled Twin Peaks room.

## 11.14 MY SIDE

**Address:** Veemkade 1000-1210
**Architect:** de Architekten Cie. (Frits van Dongen)
**Client:** Amstelland Vastgoed
**Year:** 1995

The two symmetrical identical parts of the building were already completed in 1995 as one of the first housing developments in what was a fairly desolate looking area at the time.
They are thus not included in the master plan for the Oostelijke Handelskade (now Piet Heinkade), in which the appearance of the warehouse architecture has been taken as the starting point.
The apartments – 106 owner-occupied units, most of them maisonettes of various types – were distinguished by a large number of smart devices, such as computerised heating, bath and lighting which can also be remotely controlled by telephone, touch screens for leaving messages, and video monitors next to the door bells. In fact these facilities are a precursor of the trend that was to continue in this housing district: a luxurious metropolitan housing environment, orientated towards the city and comfort. Large elements and hard materials have been used such as corrugated sheeting, glass and plaster, but also wood and stucco. The use of so many different kinds of materials in the façade was a trend in the 1990s. Later, starting with Piraeus, a more sober choice of materials came into fashion.

## 11.15 PANAMA

**Address:** Oostelijke Handelskade 4
**Architect:** B. de Greef, W. Springer / VASD ontwerpers, Ruud van Empel
**Client:** Wouter Brave, Christiaan Vos, André van Gelderen
**Year:** 1885 / 2001

Club Panama presents itself as a 'symbiosis of show, dance, diner, sex appeal and club'. This is all housed in a hydraulic power station that was built in 1885 to supply steam for the cranes on the dockside.
It was converted into an electric power station in 1899, when an extra wing was added to accommodate the boilers. In 1951 the whole complex was transformed into a rectifier, the so-called Eastern Docklands Power Station.
The style of this industrial monument is characterised by eclectic and Neo-Gothic influences, which can be seen in the arched friezes and the decorative masonry in red brick alternating with bands in natural stone.
The interior, which is still visible in the main hall, has an open roof construction with Polonceau gable roof trusses. These are thin iron trusses that hang from the ceiling, named after the engineer Camille Polonceau, who first used this type of truss in the construction of the Paris-Versailles railway in 1839.
The building was declared a state protected building in 2001.

## 11.16 NIEUW ARGENTINIË

**Address:** Oostelijke Handelskade 753-973
**Architect:** Rob Krier, Breitman & Breitman
**Client:** Stadgenoot
**Year:** 2011

The last wagon of the Oostelijke Handelskade train stood in the shed for a long time. The first design for the building was by the architect Koen van Velsen. The massive character of this complex and the fact that it only contained owner-occupied apartments in an area that otherwise showed little signs of life at the time were probably the factors which caused such a stagnation in the pre-building sales that it was decided not to go ahead with the plan. It was replaced by a new plan, commissioned by Het Oosten housing corporation (now Stadgenoot) and drawn up by Rob Krier (Luxembourg) and Marc Breitman (France). The programme now consists for 70 per cent of smaller rented accommodation in the free market sector, and for 30 per cent of rented council flats and a hostel for young drifters.
The style of the design is a mixture of robust nineteenth-century warehouse style with a sort of fin-de-siècle style, with dominant arched shapes in the façade, Neo-Classical railings in front of the windows, and overhanging verandas. In this sense the design is not entirely in line with the severe architectural idiom of the new buildings that were planned for this strip.

## 11.17 PAKHUIS WILHELMINA

**Address:** Veemkade 570-598, Groenhoedenveem 2-30
**Architect:** CASA architecten
**Client:** Stichting Wilhelmina
**Year:** 1892 / 1967 / 2004

Built in 1892 by the Vriesseveem company and drastically renovated in 1967, the Pakhuis [Warehouse] Wilhelmina was squatted in the 1980s by artists, architects and musicians, who formed a close-knit community. A more commercial exploitation had to be found in the form of a foundation to guarantee the survival of the complex and to pay for the renovation. There are a venue/bar for pop music, a gamelan house, design and woodwork shops, and a good deal more.

## 11.18 CHICAGO

**Address:** Waagdragerhof 2-198
**Architect:** Rapp+Rapp
**Client:** Ontwikkelingscombinatie Nieuw Amerika (Het Oosten, Ymere, Johan Matser)
**Year:** 2006

Chicago is the name of one of the three complexes in the Nieuw Amerika planning zone. This apartment complex comprises both rented and owner-occupied apartments and has been built in a U-shape with steel walkways beside and half over the Pakhuis Wilhelmina. The overhanging volumes caused a good deal of commotion among the residents of the Pakhuis Wilhelmina. The artists who have their studios in that warehouse were seriously worried about the fire risk: the old and new buildings would be less than three metres apart, resulting in a chimney effect if fire were to break out. This led to a number of court hearings, after which a temporary cessation of building activity was announced. After a package of new agreements, building activity was resumed.

## 11.19 BOSTON AND NIEUW AUSTRALIË

**Address:** Veemkade 562-568, Purperhoedenveem 2-140, Groenhoedenveem 1-139, Piet Heinkade 215-225
**Architect:** DKV architecten
**Client:** Ontwikkelingscombinatie Nieuw Amerika (Het Oosten, Ymere, Johan Matser)
**Year:** 2005

Like the Pakhuis Amerika, the old Pakhuis Australië was originally built in 1893–1895 for the Blaauwhoedenveem company. When fire broke out in 1948, the Amerika was completely gutted; Australië was seriously damaged, but could later be restored. DKV, the architects of the new Boston building, originally planned to wrap up the old building by erecting the new one over it. However, during the building stage the old warehouse caught fire again in 2003, and this time it was completely destroyed. The planning stage was so advanced by now that it was decided to reconstruct the Australië as it had been before 1948 so that the DKV plans could be implemented with as few alterations as possible. The new building has a U-shaped mass which is connected to the old building by glass volumes. The plinth is completely filled with business units. On top of them is a shared garden on a slope, which yields an unusual perspective. The owner-occupied and rented apartments in both parts are like lofts. The clustering of the shafts for piping and cabling has resulted in ground plans that can be divided up in all kinds of ways. The window fronts are completely foldable so that an internal balcony can be created.

## 11.20 DETROIT

**Address:** Veemkade 366-560, Purperhoedenveem 7-15, Withoedenveem 8-16
**Architect:** awg architecten
**Client:** Ontwikkelingscombinatie Nieuw Amerika (Het Oosten, Ymere, Johan Matser)
**Year:** 2006

Luxury beside the IJ — this complex offers it. The Detroit residents have at their disposal a health club with swimming pool, two saunas and a fitness area, laundry area and two guest rooms for the guests of the residents. There is a shopping and dry cleaning service, and various modern domestic devices have been incorporated in the apartments. Vesteda, which lets apartments in the free market sector, lets these apartments and has its office on the ground floor. The volume on the waterfront side follows the long wall of warehouses for its entirety, while the side facing the railway line seems to be more of a self-contained object. That is what Christian Rapp had in mind in the urban development plan that was made for the ensemble of three complexes called Nieuw Amerika. Rapp also devised a rule, following the example of New York, to determine the maximal building volume per storey: 100 per cent on the ground floor, 70 per cent in the middle, and 50 per cent on top. This has been followed by awg architecten by letting the sturdy volume, clad in dark brick with hardly any grouting, effect a transition from a rectangular to a wedge-shaped form to ensure optimal daylight for the apartments. There are roof terraces on the second and sixth floors.

## 11.21 DE LOODSEN

*The Kunstplein has been wedged between the buildings on the east side. Bureau KKEP devised* Ledwork*, a large number of solar-powered lamps that are incorporated in the paving of the square. By day the sun charges the battery, while at dusk and in the night the lamps flicker, though not in sync, resulting in a constantly changing artistic pattern.*

**Address:** Veemkade 232-364, Veembroederhof 1- 287, 4-366, Piet Heinkade 183, 199-201, 211
**Architect:** Köther en Salman Architekten, hvdn architecten,Wingender Hovenier Architecten
**Client:** Ymere, Hopman Interheem Groep
**Year:** 2006

The ensemble known as De Loodsen [The Sheds] consists of two buildings like railway carriages on the waterfront with a higher part, and four individual towers, each 35-metres high, on the south side. The urban development plan is by Köther en Salman Architekten. They also designed a 'carriage' and a tower block, as did hvdn architecten. Wingender Hovenier designed two towers. They have all been named after exotic commodities: Cocoa and Cotton for the carriages, Tea, Coffee, Cinnamon and Pepper for the tower blocks.
Atria with a glass roof facing the water provide access to the entrances of the carriage complexes. The atria are open to the public but are closed at night – a model imported from the USA. There are business units in the plinth and tended apartments in both the private and the social sector as well as owner-occupied apartments above them.
The master plan for the entire strip along the former Oostelijke Handelskade opted for austere external walls, which ruled out hanging balconies. However, small industrially designed, staggered balconies were possible in the side walls of some of the apartment blocks of this complex.

## 11.22 PAKHUIS DE ZWIJGER

*Café-restaurant De Zwijger, which is open all day, is located in the underground corridor of the building and affords a view of the bridge and the IJhaven. The interior design tried to preserve the robust character of the building as far as possible. The bar has been folded between the octagonal columns.*

*De Zwijger owes its name to the holding of a competition among the personnel of the Maatschappij Blaauwhoedenveem-Vriesseveem. What motives led to the selection of this particular suggestion are not known.*

*Nine blue mosaic sheets have been attached to the east side with the names of the places where the Maatschappij Blaauwhoedenveem-Vriesseveem, the owner of the premises at the time, had its offices.*

**Address:** Piet Heinkade 179
**Architect:** J. de Bie Leuvelink Tjeenk and K. Bakker/ Architectenbureau J. van Stigt
**Client:** Maatschappij Blaauwhoedenveem-Vriesseveem / Stadsherstel Amsterdam
**Year:** 1934 / 2006

Because of its status as a preserved historic building, De Zwijger has managed to hold on to its old silhouette in spite of the hole created by the Jan Schaeferbrug. The De Zwijger cool store, designed by the architects J. de Bie Leuvelink Tjeenk and K. Bakker and completed in 1934, has a no-nonsense expressionist style and was already a famous example of modern architecture in its day. It was one of the most modern cool stores where perishable foodstuffs such as meat could be kept for longer periods. The supporting construction consists of a skeleton of reinforced concrete with octagonal columns and mushroom floors to carry a lot of weight. The façade is clad with half-brick masonry for extra isolation and to prevent concrete rot.
De Zwijger was squatted in the 1980s, after which it was used primarily for wild parties and as a rehearsal place for bands. Because of the insulating thick walls, musicians like Loïs Lane and Herman Brood could let rip. For a while there was talk of demolishing the complex because the foundations did not seem to be in order after the bridge had been driven through the building. At this the Cuypers Association asked for the building to be declared a state protected historic monument, and the application was accepted. After intensive feasibility studies by the De Zwijger Foundation and many consultations with the local authority, it was decided to preserve the premises and convert them into a multimedia centre. André van Stigt and Stadsherstel Amsterdam carried out the renovation. Openings were made in the façade on the north side to let in daylight. Cultuurfabriek, Waag Society, the Amsterdam Art Fund, Salto Broadcasting Amsterdam and the Mediagilde are the new users.

## 11.23 JAN SCHAEFERBRUG

*The Jan Schaeferbrug is named after the leader of the Partij van de Arbeid (PvdA) in Amsterdam, who was a councillor (including Urban Renewal) from 1978 to 1986. Building activity had more or less come to a standstill just before his period of office, and only a few hundred homes were still built. Four years later more than 8,000 were being built in one year. He is famous for the immortal words: 'You can't live in bullshit'.*

**Address:** Piet Heinkade / Javakade
**Architect:** Venhoeven CS
**Client:** Amsterdam Local Authority
**Year:** 2001

The Jan Schaeferbrug has been constructed to optimise access to the 1,200 metre long Java island. Once it had been decided to make the bridge land on the city side in the Kattenburgerstraat, it had to go right through the De Zwijger warehouse. Contrary to what was originally supposed, the foundations of the warehouse were strong enough for the construction.
The winning design in the multiple design competition organised by the local authority was by the architect Ton Venhoeven. The bridge had to have components that could be dismantled to allow large sailing vessels to pass during the SAIL festival, which is held once every five years. Each of the two removable parts weighs 200 tons. When necessary they are taken away on pontoons. Pedestrians, cyclists and motorised traffic enter the bridge from separate access ramps, but meet one another on the bridge. The construction is very flat and almost without vertical elements. High tech materials were used, and the Jan Schaeferbrug has earned itself the nickname The Lizard.

*To give the Veemkade a dockland character, Esticon concrete sheets have been used for the quay. The covering layers have bee scrubbed to make the basalt visible. The sheets have a galvanised, hot-rolled edge. The large square tiles already fill a surface area of 10,000 m2.*

## 11.24 PAKHUIS AFRIKA AND HUYS AFRIKA

**Address:** Oostelijke Handelskade 19
**Architect:** KCAP Architects & Planners, Villanova
**Client:** Oosterveen, Heijmans IBC Projectontwikkeling
**Year:** 1913 / 2009

Huys Afrika [Africa House] has been built in front of and above Pakhuis Afrika [Africa Warehouse]. The new building is to accommodate 52 apartments, while business units have been developed in the warehouse – now rented by the Ymere housing corporation. It was built in 1913 as a cool store, but the construction was not ideal: the walls started to rust and there was too little insulation. All the same, the so-called mushroom floors – concrete columns that fanned out in the floor and could carry a lot of weight – earned it a place as a state protected historic building. In 2003 the warehouse was squatted and in the two following years it became more and more of a cultural breeding ground. The squatters made a name for themselves with the recurrent cultural event 'Damoclash'. In the spring of 2005 the premises were evacuated because of the risk of fire, after which work on the new building could commence.
The columns and staircases of the new building poke through the warehouse. The architects wanted the prefabricated concrete façade with its various colour nuances to refer to the rusty colours of the quays.

## 11.25 PAKHUIS AMSTERDAM

**Address:** Jollemanhof 9-17
**Architect:** Meyer en Van Schooten Architecten, Urban Office (Madir Shah), Antarctic (Antoine van de Vijver)
**Client:** Konig & Cie
**Year:** 1999

The Nederlands Interieur Collectief commissioned the renovation of this old warehouse – which was called Pakhuis Azië [Asia Warehouse] at the time – in 1999. The wooden shutters were replaced with glass, and voids and breaches were implemented inside to make the warehouse suitable as a modern office space.
By now the warehouse has been let to various parties, including Greenpeace. The ground floor is the site of restaurant Fifteen, where underprivileged youths can be trained as chefs, a scheme based on a project by the English chef Jamie Oliver. The original dark cast-iron columns have been given a central role in the interior.

## 11.26 GIBRALTAR

**Address:** Jollemanhof 22-152
**Architect:** Claus en Kaan Architecten
**Client:** IBC/Heijmans, Ymere
**Year:** 2004

The development of the Piet Heinkade was based on the principle of preserving the atmosphere of the huge and solid warehouses as far as possible. This meant that the new building must look like a block that is lived in, but not like domestic apartments. The Gibraltar complex contains 66 rented council flats and 6 owner-occupied business units on the ground floor, but from outside it looks like an office block. The apartments do not have any balconies or terraces. Three façades have been composed of floor-to-ceiling prefab elements in a sand-coloured concrete. The north wall, where galleries give access to the apartments, is entirely of glass. This allows a maximum of light to enter, because the Pakhuis Amsterdam stands right in front of it up to the fifth floor.
In allocating the council flats, the Ymere housing association experimented with a new procedure. Applications were pre-selected by lifestyle on the basis of an extensive questionnaire. The future residents had to make a deliberate choice to live in this block. One year after completion, the caretaker had still not received a single complaint about other residents. Of course, there are some residents with a will of their own: one has ventured to hang bright red geraniums in his window, a cheerful interruption to the minimalist look of the façade.

## 11.27 HUYS AZIË

**Address:** Jollemanhof 5-7 and 8-20
**Architect:** KCAP Architects & Planners
**Client:** IBC/Heijmans, Rodamco
**Year:** 2005

Huys Azië [Asia House], not to be confused with Pakhuis Azië (which has been renamed Pakhuis Amsterdam), is the counterpart of Huys Europa in terms of urban design. The complex consists of two buildings. An L-shaped low-rise three-storey block stands on top of two underground levels of parking lots. The heavy dimensions of the steel H-profiles that frame the wall-length rows of windows give the building the appearance of a stripped old warehouse. A brick volume leans against it that looks fairly massive at ground level, but which grows increasingly slender as it rises because of the 'evaluative window articulation', that is, the fact that the windows grow steadily larger storey by storey.

## 11.28 HUYS EUROPA

**Address:** Piet Heinkade 141-173, Jollemanhof 1-4
**Architect:** de Architekten Cie. (Branimir Medić, Pero Puljiz)
**Client:** IBC/Heijmans, Rodamco
**Year:** 2005

This is the former site of the Huys Europa, which formed a 200-metre wall together with its Asian and African counterparts. While the latter have been renovated, the Huys Europa was demolished in 1999 after several renovations. The robust façade elements of the new Huys Europa are an attempt to blend with the large-scale maritime atmosphere of the waterfront. The plinth and four floors of office space are rented by the Ahold food concern. The upper storeys contain twelve apartments, each with a floor space of almost 200 m2. The façades are as transparent as possible thanks to the glass window fronts and glass sheeting of the outdoor areas, resulting in an optimal view. The transfer of the Ahold top management to the South Bank of the IJ and not to the South Axis, for instance, was a deliberate choice, influenced by the combination of housing, business and cultural facilities on the Piet Heinkade.

## 11.29 PIET HEIN BUILDINGS

**Address:** Piet Heinkade, Veemkade
**Architect:** Hans van Heeswijk architecten, Dick van Gameren Architecten
**Client:** Piet Hein Buildings bv (Slavenburg's Bouwbedrijven among others)
**Year:** 2013

After a failed development, the gaping hole in the line of buildings on the Piet Heinkade is now being filled by a touring car terminal for the Amsterdam Passenger Terminal with an office complex above it. The waterfront terminal designed by Hans van Heeswijk is a large multipurpose hall with glass façades. Passengers can transfer directly to the buses here. The office complex comprises four blocks, each with its own appearance and choice of materials. One of them was designed by Dick van Gameren. A two-level car park is being constructed below ground level. The side of the building facing the city already has a taxi rank and a loop for the tram to turn. The ambition is to obtain an A energy classification for the whole complex.

## 11.30 IJTOREN DEXIA

*The clean soil that is removed during the drilling of the tunnels for the North-South Line is being used to make the IJhaven less deep. It is fairly deep at the moment, leading to little or no life on the river bed. It is better for nature if the water is shallower, because that allows more light to reach the river bed. That means more plant life, which is also beneficial for the stock of fish. An added advantage is that it reduces the cost of making mooring facilities for inland vessels and houseboats.*

**Address:** Piet Heinkade 55
**Architect:** HOK
**Client:** Amplan
**Year:** 2002

This office block was originally developed for Bank Labouchere and was also to be named after the client, but after the takeover of the Belgian Dexia Bank it looked as though it was going to become the Dexia Tower. After several negative affairs, however, Dexia Bank had to cut back and the new office on the bank of the IJ was no longer needed. Other parties – a firm of solicitor, an insurance broker, the head office of Philips Consumer Lifestyle – rented a floor in the tower block. It is known as IJtoren even though the other building at the end of the Veemkade was also called by the same name.
The 90-metre IJtoren is the tallest building on the South Bank of the IJ. The austere glass façade of the anonymous office block was designed by Larry Malcic of the US-based firm HOK (Hellmuth, Obata + Kassabaum), one of the largest firms of architects in the world, which also designed the adjacent Passenger Terminal.
As in the case of the more recent Mövenpick Hotel, there were serious protests from the Association of Friends of the Amsterdam Inner City because of the obstruction of the historic lines of vision from the centre to the harbour and the IJ.

## 11.31 PASSENGER TERMINAL AMSTERDAM

*Situated only 25 kilometres from the open sea and with the high speed train as a gateway to the rest of Europe, the terminal is an attractive place for cruisers to moor. The growth of the number that stop in Amsterdam is so large that there are plans to build an extra terminal in the western area of the docks.*

**Address:** Piet Heinkade 27
**Architect:** HOK
**Client:** Amsterdam Port Authority, Amsterdam Local Authority, NS Stations
**Year:** 1999

*The major nautical event SAIL is held on and around the IJ. For five days the Amsterdam harbour is filled with a variety of vessels: tall ships, replicas, naval vessels and sailing heritage. Various performances and activities are organised as well. The most recent Sail, in 2010, attracted 1.5 million visitors to the IJ. The first SAIL was organised in 1975 in connection with the 700th anniversary of Amsterdam. The event was such a success that it was decided to repeat the event in 1980 and every five years afterwards.*

The Amsterdam Passenger Terminal (PTA) was built in 1999, making it one of the first of the new projects on the Piet Heinkade. The main function of the building is the reception of passengers from ocean cruisers in Amsterdam. Like the IJtoren Dexia, it was designed by Larry Malcic from the US-based firm of architects Hellmuth, Obata + Kassabaum (HOK). The architect has emphasised the nautical appearance of the building with its pronounced wave-shaped form. That form also indicates that this is a point of intersection between water and land. Since the façade is mainly glass, each of the three decks – Main Deck, Promenade Deck, and Panorama Deck – offers a panoramic view of the IJ.

## 11.32 MÖVENPICK HOTEL

**Address:** Piet Heinkade 11-19
**Architect:** Claus en Kaan Architecten
**Client:** Amplan
**Year:** 2006

Mövenpick Hotels & Resorts has various branches in Europe and the Middle East. The chain has three hotels in the Netherlands, including this 410-room hotel wedged between the Passenger Terminal and the Muziekgebouw. The building was originally planned to be considerably lower than the IJtoren Dexia, which would have created a gradual increase in height between the Muziekgebouw, the hotel and the office block. Under pressure from the client, however, the hotel was built almost as tall as the tower block, resulting in a more static composition from the Central Station than had been intended in the master plan.

The height of the façade strips, in glass, green granite, white marble and white concrete, does not correspond to that of the storeys. So this is not a case of form follows function, but one with a Modernist twist.

## 11.33 PEDESTRIAN BRIDGE OVER THE ZOUTHAVEN

*After redevelopment, the part of the Oostelijke Handelskade between the Muziekgebouw and Panama has been given a new name: Piet Heinkade, which later turns into the Piet Heintunnel. It is named after one of the greatest maritime heroes of the Netherlands, who won naval victories in various parts of the world during the era of the Dutch East India Company and its West Indian counterpart. Piet Hein lived from 1577 to 1629. His fame today is partly due to the song about him that J.P. Heije wrote in 1844:*

*Did you hear about the silver fleet,*
*The silver fleet of Spain?*
*They had many Spanish coins aboard,*
*And apples of Orange.*

*Piet Hein!, Piet Hein!,*
*Short is the name, Piet Hein,*
*His deeds are great,*
*His deeds are great,*
*He did win the Silver Fleet,*
*He did win, did win the Silver Fleet.*
*He did win the Silver Fleet.*

**Address:** Piet Heinkade 1
**Architect:** Hans van Heeswijk architecten
**Client:** Amsterdam Development Corporation (OGA)
**Year:** 2004

The bridge over the Zouthaven connects the through road and the tram stop with the Muziekgebouw. The design refers to the pedestrian bridges that used to be a common sight between the ships and the quay, but upside down. It is a suspension bridge made of a fan-like steel tensile construction with 21 cross trusses, whose tension cables extending generously under the steep bridge deck. The tension cables run along the sides and underneath the bridge but cannot be seen above the bridge deck. There is therefore nothing to block the view from the bridge. Because it was difficult to predict the vibration with such an elegant construction, tests were conducted after completion to determine whether and where absorbers were required. It is still quite an experience to cross the bridge when it is windy or raining.

## 11.34 MUZIEKGEBOUW AAN 'T IJ

**Address:** Piet Heinkade 1
**Architect:** 3xNielsen
**Client:** Amsterdam Port Authority
**Year:** 2005

The Muziekgebouw can certainly be regarded as the most striking new building on the South Bank of the IJ, not only because of the quality of the design, but above all because of the function (centre for contemporary music) on this location in the city. While in other cities such unique locations are barely able, if at all, to withstand the pressure of commercial investors, the Amsterdam local authority has implemented a cultural centre here that has given a clear impulse to the image of the South Bank.
In the 1990s the undeveloped land at the top of the Piet Heinkade was used by the Traffic Department as a depot for cars that had been towed away.
It was not a pretty sight, on the edge of the city behind the railway line, and it was also used as an illegal prostitution zone.
Now the cultural élite of the city use the pedestrian bridge to reach the Muziekgebouw and Bimhuis, which opened in 2005, for a concert or a visit to the café-restaurant Star Ferry with a large terrace overlooking the water.
After a multiple study assignment, the design by the Danish firm of architects 3XN was chosen as the most suitable for the location in 1997. The potential of the site has been used to the full by making every side of the building equally important. Moreover, the plan was able to manage with the limited budget of € 60 million.

The main concert hall consists of a functional concrete box with a seating capacity of 729 or a standing capacity of 1500. The concrete walls were cast in situ in the work to provide optimal soundproofing from the noise of trains and other traffic. The apparently arbitrary seams were in fact designed beforehand with the aid of a computer.
The walls inside the hall itself are clad with Canadian maple. A genuinely innovative feature of the hall is the moveable ceiling, which makes it possible to create a different volume depending on the type of concert and thereby to influence the length of resonance of the sound waves.
The façade round the concrete box is like a transparent shell. The space between the façade and the concert hall is designed for all public functions, as well as for music company offices. The floors on each level are covered with untreated Brazilian hardwood. Daylight reaches deep into the building through the glass exterior, and after dark the Muziekgebouw is a beacon on the South Bank of the IJ.

## 11.35 BIMHUIS

*The red brown tile used to cover the plinth, devised by the architects of the IJtoren Dexia, was later also applied to the neighbouring premises in consultation with the supervisor of the area and the other architects. The idea was to emphasise the elongated shape of the area and to achieve unity at ground level. Each of the building has an expression of its own above the shared plinth.*

**Address:** Piet Heinkade 1
**Architect:** De Vries Bouwma architecten
**Client:** Amsterdam Port Authority
**Year:** 2005

On the south side of the Muziekgebouw a black volume like a shoe box sticks out of the façade. This is the Bimhuis, with a small concert hall and bar to cater for an audience of around 500. On the inside the hall is like a peep-box, with a large window behind the stage offering a view of the railway line and the historic centre. The hall and bar have been designed in such a way that the two connecting areas can be divided up in various ways by means of partitions that can be left open or closed.

TERRACE AT THE MUZIEKGEBOUW

# 12. OOSTERDOK

In the seventeenth century the Oosterdok was a bustling part of Amsterdam; it was the base of the navy and the Dutch East India Company ships, and many wharves were established there. The silting up of the IJ, however, made it increasingly difficult for large vessels to reach it. The 'Canal King' Willem I ordered the construction of the Oosterdoksdijk in 1832 to ensure moorings of sufficient depth in the city.
Nevertheless, the harbour moved further eastwards in the following decades and the Oosterdok became the scene of other activities. The Central Station and a marshalling yard were built, and the Oosterdokseiland was consolidated to form a location for the sorting department of the Dutch Post Office. Today only the Maritime Museum and the dock for historic vessels still recall the maritime past of this site.
In the 1990s the local authority decided to draw the area into the city as part of the plan to develop the South Bank. Erick van Egeraat's master plan created a contemporary link with the centre. The radial structure that is typical of the ring of canals has been extended to divide the islands into six plots. The building heights of these plots gradually rise from the Central Station to the height of the tower of the former postal building. The rhythm of the inner city of Amsterdam has also been followed in the guidelines for windows and the choice of materials.
The programme of the Oosterdokseiland is highly urban. The main branch of the Public Library is the major attraction, but the Amsterdam Conservatory and the City Inn Hotel with congress facilities, shops, catering and offices all contribute. The apartment blocks ensure that the area remains alive outside office hours.
Sustainability criteria that go beyond the norms prescribed by legislation have been applied to all the buildings. The application of underground heat and cold storage and the use of solar panels form one of the main systems to supply the island with energy.
North of the tracks beside the De Ruyterkade, the historical buildings have been left intact, or new buildings have been added where necessary. The maritime environment of the Oosterdok around the NEMO and the Maritime Museum preserves the character of a nautical zone for ships with a historic character.

## 12.1 IJ TUNNEL

**Architect:** E. Hartsuyker
**Client:** Amsterdam Local Authority
**Year:** 1968

The IJ tunnel links the northern district of Amsterdam with the rest of the city via the centre. The tunnel was a long time in the making. Designs for a bridge over the IJ were already made in the nineteenth century, and later the possibility of a tunnel emerged as well. After decades of debating the merits of a bridge or a tunnel, in 1952 the local authority finally took the plunge and opted for the tunnel. Another sixteen years were to pass before the tunnel could actually be used. It was mainly financial factors that played a role in all this: there was a shortage of resources, and the government gave priority to the Schellingwouderbrug (1957) and the Coentunnel (completed in 1966). The completed IJ Tunnel, which was opened by Queen Juliana in 1968, is a two-lane dual carriageway and is 1,039 metres long. It is easy to recognise the tunnel on the North and the South Banks by the characteristic double funnel-shaped ventilation shafts designed by Enrico Hartsuyker, who later designed the entrances to the Zeeburgertunnel. On the South Bank they stand next to the bridge between the Stationseiland and the Piet Heinkade; on the North Bank they are situated behind the Sixhaven. The architect, who was born in Genoa, drew his inspiration for the towers from chimneys, bell-towers and other towers that are often seen on Italian public buildings. Beneath the towers are operating posts with direct access to the tunnel. The tunnel tubes were renovated in the 1980s, when a further operating post was added. Given the compactness of the programme, it is designed like the saloon of a ship.

*For the attentive passer-by: the eastern underpass between the Zouthaven and the Kop Dijksgracht is accompanied by acoustic art specially composed for this location.*

## 12.2 CENTRAL CLIMBING WALL

**Address:** Dijksgracht 2
**Architect:** Loof & van Stigt
**Client:** Rock Steady Haarlem
**Year:** 1996

The function of this climbing wall finds very direct expression in the form and choice of materials. The outer walls of the tilted box, clad with polyester and aluminium-coloured corrugated sheeting, are almost entirely closed, which enables optimal use to be made of the walls sloping forwards and backwards. Climbing routes of different levels of difficulty can thereby be created.
The Building Inspectorate was strongly opposed to the object at first on the grounds that it would result in 'an unacceptable fragmentation of the public space'. However, a building permit was eventually issued because of the temporary character of the object. It has no foundations and was built in a mere twelve weeks. It was initially placed on the side of the tracks beside the water, but with the development of the eastern side of the De Ruyterkade, it was loaded onto a pontoon in a single night in 2003 and transferred to its present, equally temporary location.

## 12.3 HANNEKES BOOM... SINDS 1662

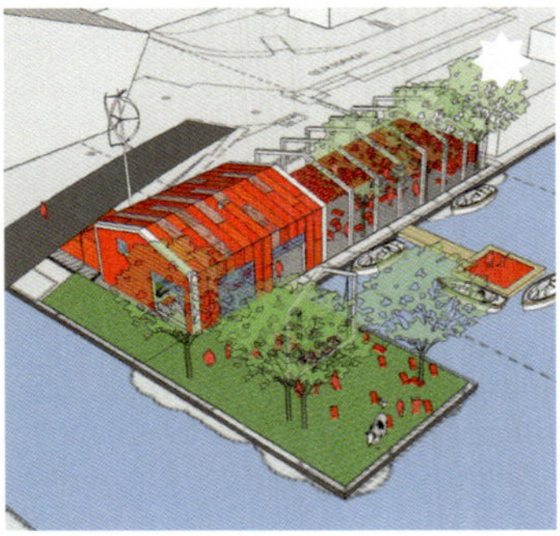

**Address:** Kop Dijksgracht
**Architect:** V2A architectuur & stedenbouw
**Client:** Stichting Hannekes Boom...sinds 1662
**Year:** 2011

The Amsterdam local authority organised a competition for a temporary catering establishment on the Kop Dijksgracht. A varied group of entrepreneurs won, each of whom was to implement a part of the plan. The result is a café-restaurant specialised in sausages, Spanish flamenco evenings and lessons, and nautical activities aimed at water recreation along the quay. The name Hannekes Boom appears on a map of 1662, when there was a manned opening here in the double row of piles along the bank of the IJ to keep a check on vessels entering the city. The temporary structure with fully glazed overhead doors and a terrace will be allowed to stand for at least five years.

## 12.4 BRIDGES AROUND THE OOSTERDOKSEILAND

**Architect:** Kerste-Meijer Architecten
**Client:** Amsterdam Local Authority
**Year:** 1998 / 2005

Two new pedestrian bridges give access to the Oosterdokseiland on the east side. One of them links the NEMO and the Central Station, the other gives access to the Piet Heinkade and therefore also forms the slow traffic route for tourists from the cruise vessels.
Their design had to take into account the view from the historic city over the water. In other words, the bridges had to be as unobtrusive as possible when viewed from the side. The choice therefore fell on light steel constructions and little lighting. They are operated from a new operating post designed by the same firm of architects.

## 12.5 NEMO

**Address:** Oosterdok 2
**Architect:** Renzo Piano
**Client:** Amsterdam Local Authority, Ministry of Economic Affairs, Stichting NEMO
**Year:** 1997

The biggest roof terrace in the city with a spectacular view of the city centre — that is the top deck of the NEMO science museum. This urban square towers above the spot where the traffic of the IJ Tunnel goes underground, and makes exactly the same angle with the surface of the water as the tunnel does. In this respect, NEMO and the tunnel mirror one another.
The tunnel was the most important source of inspiration for the Italian architect Renzo Piano, whose works include the Centre Pompidou in Paris and the Kensai Airport Terminal in Osaka. Many people see the volume that emerges from the water as a big ship that has suffered shipwreck in the waters of the Oosterdok. The curved volume is clad with oxidised copper plates, whose green colour goes a long way to defining the exterior of the building. The ground level façade is almost entirely covered with glass, making the copper volume seem to rise above an imaginary waterline.

## 12.6 MARITIME MUSEUM

*There are twenty floating monuments in the Nautical Quarter of the Oosterdok. These vessels destined for inland shipping provide a survey of more than a century of Dutch shipping. There are signs on the quayside with information about the history of each vessel. The fleet belongs to the members of the Amsterdam Harbour Museum Association (VMA), which is connected with the Maritime Museum. The* Christian Brunnings *is noteworthy, a steamship that was built in 1900 as an icebreaker, but was also intended as a vessel for directors, which explains the luxurious saloon with a marble fireplace.* De Amsterdam, *lying by the quay of the Museum, is a replica of the original East India Company ship that still lies buried beneath the sand off the coast of Hastings in England.*

**Address:** Kattenburgerplein 1
**Architect:** Daniël Stalpaert / Dok architecten, Rappange & Partners Architecten, Ney + Partners
**Client:** Government Buildings Department
**Year:** 1656 / 2011

While many large buildings today require several years for their completion, in the seventeenth century the architect Daniël Stalpaert managed to create 's Lands Zeemagazijn in less than nine months, as is reported on the three entrance arches on the west side. That period does not include the time required for the complex laying of the foundations in the water, but still.
The building was used as a warehouse for the storage of items for the Admiralty vessels, whose task it was to defend the territory and merchant fleet of the Dutch Republic. The items in storage were therefore not confined to shipping equipment, but also included arms and cannon. Every side of the building stands in the water to facilitate loading and unloading.
The Zeemagazijn was built in the same time and style – Dutch Classicism – as the Palace on Dam Square, but its decoration is considerably less exuberant given its warehouse function. The openings through which goods were hoisted inside can still be seen. The layer of plaster was only added at the end of the eighteenth century during one of several renovations. The building was used by the navy until the late 1960s, after which it acquired its present function as a Maritime Museum.
The building is being restored and the courtyard roofed to enable a new display of the collection. Liesbeth van der Pol, who designed the museum depot, is working on the redesign of the museum. The Brussels structural design engineer and designer Laurent Ney devised the transparent glass covering; the shape of the narrow supporting trusses is based on features from old shipping maps. Given the history of the building and the fact that it is one of the few examples of a seventeenth-century courtyard that are open to the public, the Historic Buildings and Archaeology Department of the Amsterdam local authority viewed these plans with scepticism, but the meticulous elaboration and the reversibility of the design won its approval in the end.

## 12.7 ARCAM

*Kattenburg island in the Oosterdok accommodates a Dutch Royal Navy terrain that is not open to the public. It was transferred to the Navy after the abolition of the Admiralty in 1795. It is one of the few locations in the Netherlands that is indicated as a grey area. This is because it houses one the largest military decoding centres in the world underground – a big computer that receives and deciphers messages. Plans are regularly made for this area in the centre of the city, but for the time being the Navy has no intention of moving.*
*At the beginning of 2005 Ayaan Hirsi Ali was in hiding there for a while because of threats from Muslim fundamentalists.*

**Address:** Prins Hendrikkade 600
**Architect:** René van Zuuk
**Client:** Amsterdam Local Authority
**Year:** 2002

The Amsterdam Architectural Centre is housed in one of the new pearls beside the IJ, which was specially designed for this institute. A pavilion designed by Renzo Piano had stood on this location in the armpit of the NEMO, but was never used. The architect René van Zuuk was asked to design the renovation and extension. He adopted a radical approach: all that is left of Piano's pavilion are five columns on the ground floor and a piece of floor. The rest was demolished to create a building with a floor space four times the size and an exhibition area with a glass façade overlooking the water. The façade on the street side is almost completely covered with zinc-clad aluminium (Kalzip), which has been wrapped around the volume like a skin.

## 12.8 AMSTERDAM CONSERVATORY

**Address:** Oosterdokskade 151
**Architect:** de Architekten Cie. (Frits van Dongen)
**Client:** Amsterdamse Hogeschool voor de Kunsten
**Year:** 2008

The new Conservatorium [Conservatory] has been designed in accordance with the principles of the Japanese *engawa* model. This means that all corridors are situated outside the building. The rooms, such as the auditoria and classrooms, are indoors and are thus soundproofed against noises from outside by the corridors. By introducing as much transparency as possible into the outer walls and partitions, a lot of light can be allowed to enter the rooms inside. The transparency also invites passers-by to drop in and listen to concerts and recitals by the conservatory students.

The 'performing heart' of the building is at ground level with four auditoria: the Bernard Haitink hall (capacity: 400), the Amsterdam Blue Note hall for jazz and pop (capacity: 200), the Sweelinck hall, a recital hall with an intimate atmosphere (capacity: 120), and the Theatre hall (capacity: 50).

The façades of the upper floors of the building are made of clear, heat-absorbing glass and narrow, dark aluminium profiles. The aluminium façade is shaped like the tooth of a saw for acoustic reasons; the long parts are made of fixed clear glass, while the short ones can be opened and are coated with a prismatic foil, Radiant Colour Film. This is a multi-coloured foil that, depending on the angle from which it is viewed, reflects diverse colours from the light spectrum, from magenta to cyan-blue, orange and gold.

## 12.9 AMSTERDAM PUBLIC LIBRARY

*The Italian restaurant Va Piano is situated inside the volume of the library with a terrace on the forecourt. The rear wall of the first floor is made of glass with a view through to the library.*
*There is a theatre (capacity: 27) on the seventh floor and a branch of the self-service restaurant La Place with a terrace that affords a spectacular view of the city.*

**Address:** Oosterdokskade 143
**Architect:** Jo Coenen & Co Architekten
**Client:** Amsterdam Local Authority, MAB, OOAC
**Year:** 2007

After occupying office premises on the Prinsengracht for thirty years, the new Openbare Bibliotheek Amsterdam [OBA, Amsterdam Public Library], built to accommodate 5,000 visitors a day, with a floor space of 28,000 m2 divided over eight floors, 500 internet worksites, conference rooms, and a theatre is now one of the biggest libraries in Europe.
Who could have imagined it in 1912 when a member of the First Chamber said that 'there is probably no single institute … that contributes so powerfully to confusing the mind as the public reading room'? Almost a hundred years later, the Amsterdam local authority came up with a budget of 73.6 million euro (excluding VAT) for the building of the new library.
The former Chief Government Architect Jo Coenen, who had already designed the library on the Céramique site in Maastricht, was contracted for the design. A striking feature of the building are the large, tall voids that create an enormous sense of space. At the same time a lot of attention has been devoted to creating intimate spots so that the users can concentrate on the books and other media.
The plinth has been kept as transparent as possible to emphasise the public nature of the building. It is easy to see from outside what is going on in the children's section on level –1. The form of the building is carefully tailored to match its surroundings, so that the neighbouring buildings continue to receive enough daylight.
The exterior and entrance of the building are in shell lime stone.

Extra colour has been introduced to the building by bringing in several designers, some of them young. For instance, the toilets for the visitors on level –1 have received special attention from Neeltje ten Westenend, and a felt and silk tapestry by Claudy Jongstra hangs on the entrance wall, breathing new life into an old French knot, the *guimpe*. Letter artist Martijn Sandberg made a typographic design for the light shaft that can be seen from the lifts via a transparent rear wall. The logo on the west façade was made in bronze-coloured letters by the artist Jos Hermans on the basis of the house style of the design agency Thonik. Light artist Peter van Kempen was brought in for the lighting in the building.

## 12.10 SEA PALACE

**Address:** Oosterdokskade 8
**Year:** 1984

This replica of the Sea Palace restaurant in Hong Kong is richly decorated with oriental frills. The roof of the boat is made of green glass, which the owners hope will make the building glisten like a jewel on the water.
Opened in 1984, this was the first floating restaurant in Europe, and with 700 places was immediately the largest in Amsterdam. Tourists are a main source of income, but the Chinese community in Amsterdam also makes considerable use of this restaurant for weddings and festivities.

## 12.11 HOUSING

**Address:** Oosterdokskade
**Architect:** hvdn architecten, Maccreanor Lavington architects, Crepain Binst Architecture, Meyer en Van Schooten Architecten, Baumschlager Eberle
**Client:** MAB Ontwikkeling Nederland with Meyer Bergman
**Year:** 2012

Plots 2 and 3 on the Oosterdokseiland comprise a total of 90 rented council apartments and 210 owner-occupied ones. Each consists of two projects designed by different architects. Some of the apartments are orientated towards the water, others are at right angles to it and have a front and rear on the side streets or the inner courtyards. Architectenbureau hvdn designed the de luxe apartments on the west side of plot 2, adjacent to the square beside the hotel. The plan envisages one block of two and one block of four bays, separated by an alleyway. The trapezoid shape of the plot recurs in the ground plans. The façade with its tight rhythm is clad with dark grey natural stone. The frames and balcony railings are in copper-coloured steel, and the awnings come in a yellow-gold colour. The appearance of the apartment block designed by Gerard Maccreanor on the east side of plot 2 is determined by the horizontal concrete parts and the rectangular upright panels, which are perforated with a foliate motif. There is room for an Asian supermarket and other amenities at ground level. Plot 3 contains the project by the Antwerp firm Crepain Binst Architecture on the west. Meyer en Van Schooten designed the elongated building on the east that is accessed from the side of the library by means of porches with short access galleries between them. Right at the eastern end of plot 6 the Austrian firm Baumschlager Eberle has designed a robust and solid apartment block.

## 12.12 CITY INN

**Address:** Oosterdoksstraat
**Architect:** Bennetts Associates Architects
**Client:** MAB Ontwikkeling Nederland with Meyer Bergman
**Year:** 2011

With terms like design and cosmopolitan, the Scottish hotel chain City Inn is setting up its first hotel in the Netherlands here. Next to the station with a view of both the IJ and the inner city, it has 550 luxury rooms and conference facilities to target both tourists and the business market. The complex consists of three volumes which follow the radial plot division of the rest of the new buildings on the Oosterdokseiland. The façade is composed of a combination of dark brick and movable panels in wood or metal. Each block will have a different colour awning behind the glass, so that the façade will produce an enhanced feeling of depth and each part of the building will have a character of its own. The entrance to the hotel lobby is on the forecourt that has been created beneath the roofing in the Oosterdoksstraat.

## 12.13 HOLLANDIA, NIJENBURG, DE ALEXANDER, ZEELANDIA, DE AMSTERDAM OFFICES

*The master plan for the new Oosterdokseiland was based on the former post office headquarters designed by Piet Elling in 1968. Together with the Central Station on the west side, the tall, narrow and long office building, whose lower distribution area had already been demolished, determined the maximal building height on the island. The idea was to reuse the high-rise building, though with a new design for the travertine-clad façade, in spite of the fact that its qualities were widely acclaimed by the circles of the conservation of monuments and the history of architecture. While awaiting its extreme makeover, the building has been used as temporary accommodation for the Stedelijk Museum, studios, and café-restaurant 11. However, the developer was unable to find a way of adapting the building to current standards and managed to obtain a general demolition permit from the local authority.*

**Address:** Oosterdoksstraat
**Architect:** Baumschlager & Eberle, Crepain Binst Architecture, Cie, (Designed by) Erick van Egeraat
**Client:** MAB Development with Meyer Bergman
**Year:** 2007–2014

The buildings on the side of the railway are mainly office blocks. Their names have a history: Hollandia was the name of a settlement in former Dutch New Guinea. The office was completed at the same time as the library and occupied by TomTom.
Nijenburg, situated on the square of plot 2 and designed by the Austrian firm of architects Baumschlager & Eberle, is named after the famous Dutch East India Company (VOC) vessel (1757–1769). Some three-quarters of the building are rented by Vodafone. The Nijenburg façades are finished with dark concrete and bronze-coloured frames.
De Alexander was designed by Crepain Binst Architecture and is situated on plot 3 north of the apartment block designed by the same firm. It is named after the VOC ship that was built in Middelburg in 1674. The materials of the façade are brick and glass.
Zeelandia will be built on plot 5, close to and north of the Conservatory, which was also designed by Frits van Dongen of the Cie. The name refers to the seven different ships that sailed under this flag for the VOC between 1598 and 1749. The exterior is brick with staggered wooden frames in the façade.
De Amsterdam on plot 6, where the sorting department of the Post Office once stood, is also named after a VOC merchant vessel. In terms of position and size, it is the flagship of the Oosterdokseiland. It was designed by Erick van Egeraat, who also drew up the master plan for the whole island.

## 12.14 DE ZEEVAART BUILDING / THE CHOCOLATE FACTORY

**Address:** De Ruijterkade 105-106
**Architect:** Y. Bijvoets Gzn
**Client:** Stichting De Chocolade-fabriek
**Year:** 1884 / 2013

Seeing, smelling, tasting and feeling chocolate and imagining that it is about 1880, the heyday of the chocolate industry: that is the theme of the Chocolate Factory. The underground 'secret' tram tunnel next to the corner building, which was built for the IJ tram but has never been used, will be renovated for that purpose. Visitors to this 'treat park' will be able to find out everything about chocolate interactively. According to the originator of the idea, children will pass through the machines in a small cart as though they were cocoa beans, and will come out at the other end like chocolates.

The richly decorated building De Zeevaart dates from the 1880s. The cellar was originally used to store ice and as a workshop, and later as a garage, travel agency and café-restaurant. There is a relief with children above the entrance on the corner – an appropriate subject given the future function of the building. The new building of the Chocolate Factory, in a historicising style that matches the corner building, will occupy De Ruyterkade 107 and 108.

## 12.15 LOFTICE

**Address:** De Ruijterkade 112
**Architect:** Bastiaan Jongerius Architecten
**Client:** Rami Amsterdam B.V.
**Year:** 2002

The design of this modern office among the row of old shipping companies is inspired by the undulating water of the IJ and by the view of the inner city and the untidy railway. The 25-metre deep block is divided into a front and a rear building, connected by an overhead bridge above the atrium. The bridge also has a constructional function: it holds the front and rear buildings together.

The plinth of the front façade is in ground blue hardstone. The façade above it is an alternation of wide glass strips and narrow hardstone strips. The rear façade is more closed up to the fourth floor, then it juts out six metres with an overhang entirely of glass with a clearly articulated dark border, orientated towards the inner city.

## 12.16 BESTEVAER BUILDING

**Address:** De Ruijterkade 115-120
**Architect:** J.J. Kanters / H.A.J. and J. Baanders
**Client:** N.V. Maatschappij tot exploitatie van het pand Bestevaer
**Year:** 1914 / 1929

This merchant's office consists mainly of a concrete skeleton that has been clad with bricks in traditional style. The ground floor is unusually high and was intended for wine storage. Bestevaer was the nickname of admiral Michiel de Ruyter and meant something like 'granddad'. He fought for the Republic of the Netherlands in the Anglo-Dutch War. A relief has been applied above the entrance with the devices of the Seven Provinces that composed the Republic at that time. The building is among the two hundred new national monuments.

## 12.17 FORMER FIRE STATION

**Address:** De Ruijterkade 145-149
**Architect:** W. Springer
**Client:** Amsterdam Local Authority, Stadsherstel Amsterdam
**Year:** 1890 / 2008

When Amsterdam set up a professional fire brigade in 1874, a growing demand for storage and fire drill facilities gradually emerged. One of the new fire stations was the 'Old Nico', designed by the assistant city architect W. Springer, which the Amsterdam fire brigade used until 1973.
The building, which is a national monument, is constructed with different colours of brick. The turrets and the classical division into main and subsidiary components give it the appearance of a fortress. Its former function can still be deduced from the carvings on the keystones above the semicircular arches on the ground floor: fire-fighting attributes and a salamander, a symbol of fire.
After the departure of the firemen – with the exception of two former firemen and an administrative assistant, who have stayed on and live in the station – the premises were taken over by artists and theatre makers. Its definitive function is not yet known.

## 12.18 ADMIRAAL DE RUYTER

**Address:** De Ruijterkade 152-154
**Architect:** Tijmen Ploeg Architecten
**Client:** Bouwfonds MAB
**Year:** 2008

This new office block consists of seven floors and an underground car park with 32 parking lots. The transparent entrance on the ground floor has 5.5 metre headroom. On the fifth floor there is a large roof terrace with a panoramic view of the IJ.
The south and east façades are very transparent because of the use of glass bays. The liver-coloured masonry on the side walls is in alternating rough and smooth brick. The masonry has been applied as prefabricated sandwich elements. The wall has a pronounced vertical character, and the atmosphere and colour blend with the surrounding buildings.

## 12.19 UNDER THE BRIDGE

**Address:** De Ruijterkade 151-157
**Architect:** Hans van Heeswijk
**Client:** Ymere, BAM, Amsterdam Local Authority
**Year:** 2009

In 1900 a stall selling pickles was still the main attraction on this location, but with the developments on the east side of the city, bridge 485 has become increasingly busy. The area underneath the bridge, however, was a risk factor in terms of public safety. That is why flexible business units were created at the crucial points with transparent façades to liven up the pedestrian routes from the Zouthaven towards the centre.

# 13. STATIONSEILAND

The building of the Central Station is sometimes called 'the biggest urban design mistake ever made in Amsterdam'. The plan for a station on the present site met with criticism on all sides in the 1860s. There were fears that the inner city would lose its prosperity if it were to be physically and visually cut off from its main source of wealth, the harbour. Until then the quay beside the Prins Hendrikkade had witnessed the bustle of the ships coming and going and the lively trade in commodities. Alternative locations were suggested, but in the end the government decided for Amsterdam and opted for the site in the IJ right in front of the Damrak in 1869. Sand from the dunes near Velsen that had been extracted during the construction of the North Sea Canal was used to create three artificial islands (Westerdok, Stationseiland, Oosterdok). No less than 9,000 wooden piles had to be driven into the ground for the foundations of the station buildings, though the work was still delayed for a few years because of subsidence. There was enormous public interest when Cuypers' station was opened in 1889. Compared with the construction of the eastern and western islands, this construction was not a bad idea in economic terms. The completion of the station turned the area around it into a metropolitan development with an enormous leap of scale: impressive buildings like the Mercury Building, the Victoria Hotel and the Church of St Nicholas rose amid the small-scale warehouses and trading houses that had originally fringed the open waterfront. Still, the relation between the city and the IJ seemed to have gone for good. In the second half of the twentieth century the back of the station was also effectively the back of the city.
With the redevelopment of the Stationseiland as part of the development of the South Bank of the IJ, the city has regained its waterfront after more than a hundred years. The Central Station as a central junction for public transport – train, tram, bus, metro, ferry – plays a major role in that development. The side facing the IJ has occupied a new position and when everything is finished it can be called a 'second front'. The area around the station is recovering its old island character with more water surrounding it. The slow traffic routes for cyclists and pedestrians beneath the station and the railway tracks are being extended. The quay of the IJ is being turned into a promenade and motorised traffic has largely been diverted underground. The inner city, the IJ and North Amsterdam are related to one another again.

# 13.1 POST OFFICE PARCELS BUILDING

**Address:** Stationsplein 5-7
**Architect:** J. Cuypers
**Year:** 1924 / 2007

The former Post Office Parcels Building has always been overshadowed by the main building of the Central Station. It was designed around 1924 by Jos Cuypers, a son of the famous architect. In the 1960s it lost its function as a parcels handling facility and was taken over by Dutch Rail. The top floor, for instance, was used by the Amsterdam Rail Sports Association. It had an archery room, a billiard room, changing room and canteen.

The building has now been renovated and given a new function. The cellar houses cycle racks, the Stationseiland and North-South Line information centre is on the ground floor, and the first, second and top floors have been converted into offices. The top floor has an unusual construction of riveted steel roof trusses. The original multicoloured masonry has reappeared from behind the layer of soot that had been deposited in the course of eighty years. The building is still modest beside the large volume of the Central Station, but some of its former glory has been restored.

## 13.2 NOORD-ZUID HOLLANDSCH KOFFIEHUIS

*On the right-hand side of the eastern entrance is the Queen's Pavilion, an extension building with a royal waiting room with richly decorated walls and a special toilet for the queen. The outside doors are very wide to allow coaches (nowadays cars) to enter.*

**Address:** Stationsplein 10
**Architect:** J.H.W. Leliman / Kentie en Partners Architekten
**Client:** Noord-Zuidhollandsche Tramweg Maatschappij
**Year:** 1911 / 2007

The Noord-Zuid Hollandsch Koffiehuis [North-South Dutch Coffee House], which stands in the water of the Stationsplein, accommodates a café and the tourist information office. It was originally the waiting room for the Noord-Zuidhollandsche Tramweg Maatschappij. Passengers travelled by boat from here to North Amsterdam, where they could change to the tram to Purmerend and Edam-Volendam.

The wooden building dating from 1911 is a beautiful example of a combination of styles. The architect J.H.W. Leliman drew on the sixteenth-century Paalhuis [House on Stilts] that stood in the Damrak and functioned as an office for the collection of eel and harbour dues. That was the source of inspiration for the row of Doric columns, the little stair tower, the upper façades and the waterside terrace. The coffee house was enlarged in 1930; in 1971 it was dismantled for the construction of the metro, and more than ten years later it was rebuilt on practically the same spot. The premises were recently extended even further and the paving around the building was also renewed. It is a foretaste of the future paving of the whole area in front of the station.

## 13.3 CENTRAL STATION / CUYPERS HALL

*Today the Central Station is a junction for all kinds of public transport: besides a station for trains to every point of the compass, there are a stop for three metro lines (four when the North-South Line is completed), eleven tram lines, more than thirty bus routes, and five ferries. With the development of the areas eastwards and westwards and the extension on the side facing the IJ, the building will acquire a very different position in relation to the one that it occupied in the nineteenth century.*

**Address:** Stationsplein
**Architect:** P.J.H. Cuypers with A.L. van Gendt / Benthem Crouwel Architekten
**Client:** Amsterdam Local Authority, NS Vastgoed, ProRail
**Year:** 1889 / 2015

The Central Station is without a doubt the most widely discussed building in Amsterdam because of its location. After it had been built, the inner city no longer enjoyed a view of the IJ. At first there was still some uncertainty as to where the station should be built. The local authority favoured a site on the Leidseplein, while central government preferred the present location. The decision was eventually taken in 1876 to go ahead with the government proposal. Building work began, and the station was opened in 1889. It was the first station in the Netherlands to be designed by an architect; previously these buildings had been designed by engineers. Cuypers was commissioned to design the building in the 'Old Dutch' style which was very fashionable at the time.
The Cuypers building is being restored to its original state and at the same time modified to meet present-day demands. The wealth of decoration of the original building will be brought back into view again wherever possible. The central concourse has been given a more spacious look by removing the floors with offices that were added later, so that the hall affords a view of the original monumental roof.

## 13.4 BIKE FLAT

**Address:** opposite Stationsplein 49
**Architect:** VMX Architects
**Client:** Amsterdam Local Authority
**Year:** 2001

With the unstoppable rise in the number of bikes in the city, a bike park has to be tackled seriously. The bike flat on the city side of the Central Station was originally supposed to be a temporary structure, but it will remain in place at any rate until the new bike facilities around the Central Station are ready.
The bike flat was designed for purely functional and practical purposes, but this remarkable construction has quickly become one of the tourist attractions of the city. More than 2,500 bicycles can be parked in this guarded facility seven days a week, twenty-four hours a day. The steel construction is 100 metres long, 14 metres wide, three levels high, roofed, and built on piles above the water. A system of ramps provides access to the different levels. The lowest level is 6 metres above water level so that the canal boats can manoeuvre properly to reach their landing stage. The bike flat was constructed in Friesland and transported to Amsterdam by water. Following its success, temporary bike parks have been constructed on the water on the other side of the station too.

## 13.5 SLOW TRAFFIC PASSAGE

**Address:** Stationsplein / De Ruijterkade
**Architect:** Benthem Crouwel Architekten, Merkx+Girod architecten, Irma Boom Office
**Client:** Amsterdam Local Authority
**Year:** 2011

A new slow traffic passage on the west side of the station forms a link between the city and the IJ. A tiled wall designed by the graphic designer Irma Boom rises in a flowing form from the floor to the ceiling on the side of the raised footpath. It shows a seascape with vessels inspired by a tiled tableau by the Royal Tichelaar Makkum ceramic company. The design begins as a recognisable hand-painted drawing and passes via a pixel drawing into abstract lines, symbolising the transition from the historic city centre to the new developments on the IJ.

## 13.6 IBIS HOTEL / ZILVEREN TOREN

**Address:** Stationsplein 49
**Architect:** Benthem Crouwel Architekten / Ruland + Partner Architekten
**Client:** Nederlandse Spoorwegen
**Year:** 1992 / 2008

The present Ibis Hotel and the Zilveren Toren were completed in the early 1990s, but their modern high tech design so close to the monumental station was not generally appreciated. While building was going on, the local authority gave its approval to the possibility of an extension, but only above the rails. The six-floor extension rests on ten columns and is connected with the rest of the hotel by glass walkways. The hotel rooms seem to float above the rails. The façades are clad with copper sheeting with a tin-plated surface. In the course of time this material will become matt, but is resistant to swarf from overhead contact wires and braking locomotives.

## 13.7 IJ HALL

**Address:** De Ruijterkade
**Architect:** Benthem Crouwel Architekten
**Client:** Amsterdam Development Corporation (OGA)
**Year:** 2014

For many visitors to Amsterdam, the Stationseiland is the gateway to the city. It is also the link between the IJ and the city centre. Hard work is going on to achieve the grandeur that goes with a gateway of that kind. To improve the situation on the side of the station facing the city, it was necessary to remove bus and car traffic from the area. Room has been created for them on the other side of the station by widening the old quay by 40 metres.
Cars will shortly drive into a sunken tunnel at level –1 beneath ground level on the side facing the IJ. Buses will stop at a new bus station on level +1, on the same level as the railway tracks.
The new IJ Hall, the second Central Station concourse, will be situated on ground level between the new bus station and the tunnel for cars. The side of the station facing the IJ and the city side will be linked by means of the three existing passenger tunnels and two new through corridors.
The new station of the North-South Line is at level –2 below the IJ Hall. It is directly connected with the existing eastern metro line to guarantee ease of switching between bus, train and metro. Two new, more accessible tram yards are being constructed on the side facing the city.
The new bus station beside the IJ will have a glass roof 360 metres long with a span of 60 metres. This will be the fourth station roof. AMSTERDAM can be seen on it in large letters from the IJ. This roof also partly covers the two Kiss & Ride loops and taxi ranks on both sides of the hall and a part of the open quay, providing a comfortable link between the ferry and the IJ Hall.

## 13.8 PIER 10

**Address:** De Ruijterkade 50A
**Architect:** J. de Meijer
**Client:** West-Frieslandlijn
**Year:** 1932

From the end of the nineteenth century on, the big international shipping companies set out from the eastern docklands. The smaller vessels with local traffic set out from behind the Central Station. Eighteen piers, each with its own office, were constructed here for that purpose. This building is the only survivor of that period. Constructed as a distribution office for the West-Friesland line in 1932, it was turned into a restaurant in 1987 and has been on the national list of conserved historic buildings since 2001. The side facing the water was built almost entirely of glass so that the management could have a good view of what was going on on the IJ. In spite of what one might think at first sight, the building is not made of concrete but of brick, which was plastered, sanded and painted afterwards. Within the framework of the expansion of the Central Station, the quay has been widened. The building has therefore been moved with a large floating trestle 17.5 metres further into the IJ and placed on new foundations. Restaurant Pier 10 has been serving a French-style cuisine for years.

## 13.9 SUPPERCLUB CRUISE

*Some hundred buses stop at Amsterdam Central Station every hour. The new bus station breaks with the system in which each bus line has its own bus stop. The dynamic bus stops will be assigned to different bus numbers depending on how busy it is.*

**Address:** De Ruijterkade, pier 14
**Architect:** Concrete Architectural Associates
**Client:** Supperclub Cruise
**Year:** 2004

The *Supperclub Cruise* moors now and then at Pier 14. This is a floating restaurant and night club where clients recline to eat. The concept already existed on a location behind the Kalverstraat, and by now there are also branches in Rome, London and Singapore, among others. The formula has here been extended to the water, for which the *Pieter Caland/Comtesse* was bought, which had been sailing through the harbour of Rotterdam since the 1960s. Queen Juliana liked to take her guests on board the *Pieter Caland* and had her own royal cabin on it.

## 13.10 HARBOUR BUILDING

**Address:** De Ruijterkade 7
**Architect:** W.M. Dudok, R.M.H. Magnée
**Client:** Scheepvaart Vereniging Noord, Amsterdam City Council
**Year:** 1965

'The local authority expects that the implementation of the plan will bring about a very great improvement in the appearance of this environment and that this part of the IJ banks will thereby become an attractive point in the harbour.' Those words were pronounced in the city council in 1953 on Dudok's design for the Harbour Authority, one of the few examples of reconstruction architecture in the centre of Amsterdam. Today the Harbour Authority is no longer very conspicuous, but its construction can be seen as having initiated the redevelopment of the South Bank of the IJ.
Willem Marinus Dudok owes his fame mainly to the Hilversum City Hall (1927) and the Bijenkorf department store in Rotterdam (1930). When he was commissioned by the Scheepvaart Vereniging Noord in 1951 to design a 'new Shipping Authority', he already had a lot of practical experience and a measure of arrogance. He designed not only a thirteen-storey complex but also a number of subsidiary buildings, a post building and a hotel, which he submitted together with a quotation for almost 17,000 guilders, an enormous sum (the equivalent of more than 7,000 euros) at the time and too ambitious for the local authority. The plan was

reduced to the original assignment.
The innovative feature of this example of postwar building is that the composite skeleton is not concealed by the tiled outer walls, but has been deliberately left in view. The façade on the top two floors, which house a restaurant and a canteen, is set somewhat back, which creates space for a terrace and leaves the steel construction in full view.

## 13.11 CHAMBER OF COMMERCE / SNS BANK

**Address:** De Ruijterkade 5
**Architect:** W. van Oostrum
**Client:** Mabon
**Year:** 1989

This shiny building was completed before there was a clear vision of the future of the South Bank of the IJ. It consists of two blocks with a surface area of 11,700 m2 parallel to the railway line, with a raised terrace in front of the entrance to the Chamber of Commerce. The building has a curious history: the architect was commissioned in the early 1980s to design an office block on this site for the N.O.G. (a predecessor of the current user, SNS Reaal Bank), and next to it a block with 105 rented council flats. The land, however, was enormously contaminated; it was the former site of a Dutch Rail gas works to provide the lighting for the Central Station. The delays involved in cleaning the ground were such that by the time the building application had been submitted, the grants for rented council housing had run out. The local authority did not waste any time in finding another tenant: the Chamber of Commerce was prepared to move to this location overlooking the IJ.
The architect deliberately chose to make the outer walls as glassy and shiny as possible. The alternation of reflecting glass and blue panels, framed between black profiles, enables the surroundings to be mirrored in the façade.

IJVEER
(Brom-)fietsers
motoren afzetten

Max. 240 personen
voetgangers/fietsers

# 14. WESTERDOKSEILAND

The former marshalling yard with old customs sheds was a disorderly peripheral area beside the IJ until not so long ago, but has now been converted into a highly urban residential and work environment. With the introduction of metropolitan functions, including the magistrate's court, the transformation is complete.
In 1999 the local authority drew up the development plan based on the design by the architect and urban planner Peter Defesche from OD205. The basic idea was to fit in with the density and diversity of functions and lifestyles that are so typical of the inner city of Amsterdam. The main concept was a very dense, varied building programme around courtyards ('cours') on the side facing the city, and a more uniform and monolithic building programme beside the water.
About 80,000 m2 of non-residential functions and 900 dwellings have been implemented on the Westerdokseiland. The apartments are mainly situated in three blocks: Westerkaap I and II, VOC Cour, and La Grande Cour. Several firms of architects worked on the elaboration of the various components, while one of them acted as coordinating architect each time.
A reasonably uniform building programme of up to seven storeys high was envisaged for the north side, to be implemented as a membrane of different sorts of brick. By setting some apartments back from the building line, it has been possible to build up to eleven storeys. The buildings on the Westerdok quay are lower. Sixty moorings for houseboats have been restored to maintain some of the old atmosphere and to match the character of the historic Prinseneiland and Bickerseiland.
All the plinths accommodate office and business units, which are used by a large variety of shops, from fashion to design furniture, architectural practices and advertising agencies, hotbeds for young creative talent and catering. The building of the voluminous IJdock on the site where the nineteenth-century building of the Water Police once stood is the western pendant to the Muziekgebouw on the other side of the Central Station.

## 14.1 FILM SET BESIDE THE IJ

**Address:** Korte Prinsengracht / Westerdokskade
**Architect:** Ineke Hilhorst, Chris Hutter
**Client:** Projectbureau Zuidelijke IJoever
**Year:** 2010

The subway between the Korte Prinsengracht and the Westerdokskade was dark and creepy. According to the *Nova* news programme, it was 'the ugliest place in the Netherlands'. The documentary maker and culture producer Ineke Hilhorst took the initiative of doing something about it. Light designer Chris Hutter illuminated the tunnel to give the shadows strong accents, as in a *film noir*, which accounts for the name 'Film set beside the IJ', also a reference to the film museum on the north side of the IJ.

## 14.2 HAN LAMMERSBRUG

**Address:** Westerdok / Westerdokskade
**Architect:** Meyer en Van Schooten Architecten
**Client:** Amsterdam Local Authority
**Year:** 2003

In view of the large number of different environmental elements (the railway line and the various different types of buildings), the architects designed the new bridge for cyclists and pedestrians as a sober, tranquil element. The bridge is 48 metres long and 5 metres wide, and has two supports in the water. With a gradient of 20 per cent, it is the steepest bridge in Amsterdam. The bridge is entirely constructed and clad in a light material: aluminium. The part that opens hangs just above the water level when it is vertical. This eliminates the need for a bascule cellar. The counterweight and the hydraulic pumps are small in size because of the light material used for the moveable part, and could therefore be concealed beneath the road surface.
Like the Jan Schaeferbrug, the bridge is named after a representative of the Partij van de Arbeid on the local council. Han Lammers was councillor for Urban Development from 1970 to 1976 and was a proponent of large-scale urban renewal, including the construction of the metro line to South-East Amsterdam.

## 14.3 LA GRANDE COUR

**Address:** Westerdoksdijk, Westerdoksplein, Westerdok, Winthontstraat
**Architect:** Meyer en Van Schooten Architecten, Heren 5, de Architekten Cie.
**Client:** City Cour Combination (Bouwfonds MAB, Smits Bouwbedrijf, Eigen Haard)
**Year:** 2007

For the density study for the southernmost part of the area, La Grande Cour, Meyer and Van Schooten kept the building programme as far as possible to the sides to ensure that, in spite of the high density, a maximal number of homes with a view could be created. With this aim in view, the higher volumes, which are only allowed in the central part, have been bent to extend over the buildings on the edge like periscopes. Almost all of the 252 apartments have a generous balcony, and there are communal roof terraces. There are business units in the plinth and an underground car park. The design of the block has been given to three firms of architects. Each part of the plan has its own 'cour' and periscope. All three firms have chosen the same purple-brown stone for the street façades, but their individual signature can be seen in the design and composition of the façades. The differences between the firms are more pronounced in the 'cours'. Heren 5 opted for a gradually sloping 'cour' with adjacent wooden terraces and trees in tubs, surrounded by azure stone façades. In the 'cour' by de Architekten Cie., the difference in level is resolved with a grand staircase. The inner façades are finished with upright aluminium panels. The 'cour' by Meyer en Van Schooten is on a gradual slope. It includes a tub with a mature tree.

## 14.4 19S RAILWAY BRIDGE / RESTAURANT OPEN

**Address:** Westerdoksplein 20
**Architect:** Joosting / de Architekten Cie. (Pi de Bruijn)
**Client:** Gerry Mekes, Floriaan Hackmann, Tristan Brinckman
**Year:** 1922 / 2008

There are only three rotating railway bridges in the Netherlands, and the bridge between the western Stationseiland and the Westerdokseiland is one of them. Because the bridge lost its function when the shunting area on the Westerdokseiland was closed, the local authority decided to give it a special catering function and organised a design competition. The jury chose the design of café-restaurant Open for its open character, the 'elegant open window area for fine weather', and the fact that the restaurant does not overshadow the bridge itself.
The construction consists of steel columns and girders. Because the floor joists at the ends of the bridge can slide, unwanted tensions in the old bridge caused by changes of temperature can be accommodated.

## 14.5 VLUCHTHAVENBRUG

**Address:** Westerdoksdijk and IJdock
**Architect:** Ney + Partners
**Client:** Projectbureau Zuidelijke IJoever
**Year:** 2012

The IJDock and the Westerdoksdijk will presently be connected not just for all types of motorised traffic, but also with a bridge for pedestrians. Architecturally the bridge is subordinated to the strong design and symbolism of the IJDock. It has been given a sober and modest design, but one of high architectural quality, as is shown in particular by the apparent simplicity of the construction of the surface, which is made of a bent steel sheet.

## 14.6 IJDOCK

*The side streets on the Westerdokseiland are named after historic sailing vessels: the Coffijboomstraat, the Leliendaalstraat, and the Winthontstraat. There were some political objections to the names because they might have been ships carrying slaves.*

**Address:** Westerdoksdijk
**Architect:** Dick van Gameren and Bjarne Mastenbroek (master plan), Dick van Gameren (coordinating architect), Zeinstra van Gelderen Architecten, Jan Bakers Architecten with Ben Loerakker, Claus en Kaan Architecten and de architectengroep
**Client:** Amsterdam Local Authority, Government Buildings Department, Wester IJDock CV (ASR Vastgoed Ontwikkeling)
**Year:** 2013

The IJDock pier was built to the west of the Central Station as a counterpart to the Muziekgebouw on the other side. This 'city in the water' has a surface area the size of two football fields and has an extensive programme of 56 apartments, commercial functions, a (partly) public underground car park, a hotel, a new office to accommodate the River Police and others, and the new magistrate's court. A passenger harbour with about sixty moorings is to be built between the building and the quay. The design was produced by an initial stage of throwing all the parts of the programme together in one pile to determine the maximal contour of the volume. Sections were cut out of this volume to keep the lines of vision from the centre to the IJ as open as possible. The volume with the prescribed voids was then broken down into five separate parts. These parts, which were elaborated by different architects, are adjacent to the IJDock inner street.
In the north-western section, Zeinstra van Gelderen architects have designed two buildings with apartments and offices. The hotel with its transparent façade was designed by Jan Bakers and Ben Loerakker and is situated next to the passenger harbour. The east is intended for the new magistrate's court and is designed by the Claus and Kaan firm of architects. Arising from the architectural brief, the courtrooms are on the side of the passenger harbour. Like the other buildings, the court building will have a transparent exterior in so far as the function of a magistrate's court permits.

## 14.7 GOEDKOOP BUILDING / NEVY

*The playboats* Meeuw, Meerkoet *and* Eend *are moored between the houseboats in the Westerdok. The three old flat-bottomed boats have been converted, two with play material and one with tables and benches. The soft floor guarantees that children can play there in safety.*

**Address:** Westerdoksdijk 40
**Architect:** Dekeukeleire en Grolle
**Client:** Reederij Voorheen Gebr. GoedKoop/LaMarque
**Year:** 1961

This striking example of down-to-earth functionalism from 1961 has managed to retain its position amid the developments around the Westerdok. The modest building was the office of the Goedkoop shipping company. This waterside location was chosen because of its central position and because the company tugs could moor in front of it. The company left in 1994, and after a succession of various temporary tenants the building was renovated and taken over by a legal practice and a design agency. Salt-water and freshwater fish dishes are served in restaurant Nevy on the ground floor.

## 14.8 VOC COUR

**Address:** Westerdoksdijk, Winthontstraat, Westerdok, Leliendaalstraat
**Architect:** MVRDV, Jeroen Schipper Architecten, Bosch Architects, Art Zaaijer
**Client:** Wodan CV (De Dageraad, Kondor Wessels, Nijhuis Bouw, Ontwikkelingsmaatschappij Apeldoorn)
**Year:** 2008

The central part of the new building in the Westerdok is about 100 metres square. It consists of almost 400 housing units and ground floor amenities, including a childcare centre. The composition of towers, walls and entrances is built around a large courtyard, the 'cour'. The courtyard itself is not open to the public, but can be seen through the glass entrances. It enhances the charm of the complex. Four firms of architects worked on the elaboration of the different buildings with different housing typologies, each with its own character. Art Zaaijer opted for dark brown brick for the façades. MVRDV alternated the glass façade of a strikingly transparent volume with layers of concrete. There are small balconies all around on each floor. Jeroen Schipper applied a liver-coloured hand-formed brick and large panoramic windows. John Bosch finished his block in industrial rough stone. The buildings have been given the names of VOC ships, such as *Bosschenhoven, Pallas, Morgenster, Barbesteyn*, and *Duyfken.*

## 14.9 LANDING STAGES FOR HOUSEBOATS

**Architect:** Bureau B+B Stedebouw en landschapsarchitectuur
**Client:** Amsterdam Local Authority, Royal Haskoning
**Year:** 2006

For decades there were houseboats moored on the city side of the Westerdokseiland. Some were legal, others illegal or temporary, but taken together they formed a tight-knit group of amphibians with private gardens on the quays. In developing the area, a large number of the houseboats have been given a place on the new landing stages with hardwood finish, specially suited to the type of boat. The boats now lie at right angles to the quay and have direct access to the landing stage and to their own metre cupboard.

## 14.10 WESTERKAAP

**Address:** Westerdoksdijk, Leliendaalstraat, Coffijboomstraat, Westerdok,
**Architect:** awg architecten, Concrete Architectural Associates, DKV, baneke van der hoeven architekten
**Client:** Hofmakerij (Amvest, Ymere)
**Year:** 2008

The tip of the most westerly part of the plan for the Westerdokseiland, Westerkaap, consists of two zones, both with buildings in predominantly red-brown brick. At the tip there is a block of eleven storeys designed by the Belgian firm with DKV and Concrete. In the lower part there are more diverse tower-like volumes grouped around three smaller courtyards. They were designed by DKV with baneke van der hoeven and awg. The whole complex comprises eight different typologies in every price category from council housing to expensive owner-occupied apartments.

The apartments right at the end of the island are striking. They are almost entirely made of glass and offer a view of both the IJ and the Westerdok, earning them the name Panorama apartments. Some of the apartments in the lower block are intended for senior citizens and those with a handicap, and are linked with a care concept.

## 14.11 HET STENEN HOOFD

*The old basalt quayside of the Stenen Hoofd is rich in ferns and is known for its large population of scaly and saxifrage ferns. The discovery of the navelwort is very unusual as this Mediterranean succulent is rare in the Netherlands.*

**Address:** Westerdoksdijk
**Year:** 1905

This unused site is a short pier that was built in 1905. Together with the storage facility that once stood here, it was used for transshipment from boat to train until the late 1960s. Foreign warships that docked in Amsterdam also used this pier as a mooring place at times.
Many plans have been made for this plot of land, from a rehabilitation centre for drug addicts to a location for luxurious tower blocks of flats, from a prison to a heliport. Partly thanks to the dedication of the Het Stenen Hoofd Foundation, consisting of residents who are concerned about the future of this harbour monument, it is now the site of many events and summer activities, such as the open air film festival Pluk de Nacht.

AVALON FELICITY
HAMBURG

LANDING STAGE AT THE BEGINNING OF THE PIET HEINKADE

PITO DINGEMANSE

# THE CITY AND THE PORT

The city of Amsterdam and the port of Amsterdam are an inextricable entity. Over the centuries there has always been change and development in the use of the port area for work and housing. Amsterdam and its port try to find the best way of using the port area.

## HISTORY

Amsterdam arose in the Middle Ages as a transshipment centre for herring and beer. The growth of the city in the Golden Age to become the centre of the world was due to the fact that the port linked Amsterdam with every part of the world. Many people are unaware that the port of Amsterdam is still one of the largest in the world, and ignorance breeds contempt. So the port must be made visible again for the people of Amsterdam. Urban development along the banks of the IJ is an outstanding opportunity for just that.
The history of the port can be seen everywhere in the city. The Rokin and the Damrak are relics of the medieval harbour, and the eastern and western islands were the dockland areas of the sixteenth century. It is not long since the cranes and ships left the Oostelijk Havengebied, which was created in the nineteenth century. By now all these areas have become a part of the city as attractive locations for housing and leisure.

## TRANSFORMATION OF DOCKLAND AREAS

Over the centuries, every dockland area has a curve of emergence and prosperity followed by recession and disuse. In such cases the areas that are left vacant, the rundown districts of the city, become available for other functions. This is where the pioneers who slowly developed these areas settled in the past, but today there is increasing large-scale, planned urban development. After the redevelopment of the eastern banks of the IJ in the 1980s and 1990s, the western banks of the IJ are now ripe for urban development. The Houthaven on the southern bank of the IJ and the shipping wharves on the northern side have lost their traditional port function and are now eligible for transformation. But there is one important difference from the Oostelijk Havengebied: the western banks of the IJ are right next to the modern port, which is expanding and thriving. The ecological effects of noise and smells extend over this area, which is why a special approach has to be developed for housing. Housing and work can be combined in a dockland area if the effects of the port are taken into account. The areas along Amsterdam's waterfront are perfectly suitable for urban development. The relocation of industries automatically comes up in response to the environmental effects. However, moving a modern port is not only very expensive, but it also makes a claim on the scarce green land in the North Sea Canal area. So other solutions to achieve a better match between the port and urban development are more promising.

## MINERVAHAVEN

The implementation of urban transitional zones brings the city closer to the port. Like the earlier examples of the Houthaven and the NDSM site, Minervahaven, which is situated closer to the active port, was also characterised by a decline in port functions. This zone between the port and the city became obsolete and was in danger of becoming a run-down district. After the first pioneers had already settled in the area, the Port of Amsterdam took the initiative of drawing up a plan to revitalise Minervahaven based on the premise that its buildings and appearance should match those of the city. The activities of Minervahaven are still connected with the port, which rules out the possibility of building housing there. This strategy has been very successful. The area now targets small businesses for whom the proximity of the port is an attraction. The view, sound and smell of the port are a source of inspiration instead of a source of nuisance. Along with the creative industry, restaurants and other cultural facilities are also setting up in Minervahaven, resulting in a vital buffer zone. The area has become a part of the city, and at the same time it is a link with the port. You have a fantastic view of the port activities from the Haparandadam and the Danzigerpier.

## ENVIRONMENTAL LIMITS

A second way of bringing the port and the city closer together is the legislation and regulations in the field of noise and other environmental aspects. The noise contours of the port activities extend far beyond the Houthaven and the NDSM site. Those noise limits are now decisive and constitute a limiting factor. In practice, however, few people are bothered by noise from the port, at least in the daytime. The situation is different at night, because the port functions 24 hours a day. The big difference in the perception of noise from the port in the daytime and at night calls for special regulations like those applied in Hamburg in the HafenCity project. The principle adopted there was that the noise from the port is mainly heard at night, so the regulations should target norms relating to the rooms where people sleep. By orientating bedrooms on the side where the noise is less, and by means of intelligent insulation with fresh air, a pleasant housing climate has been created close to the port of Hamburg. Amsterdam could adopt creative measures of this kind too. The challenge of the port of Amsterdam lies mainly in measures that concern smell.

## SUSTAINABILITY

In the long term a cleaner and quieter port is the solution. Sustainability is an important criterion in the port too. A cleaner and quieter port along the western banks of the IJ can be achieved by innovation on the part of the companies that are already there or through restructuring. Large-scale restructuring of port areas is not so common. Restructuring entails high costs and if the areas are situated close to the city, alternative functions are the obvious choice.
But when the nautical basic conditions are still excellent, the continuation of the port functions is a sustainable alternative. The water is deep enough, there is enough land, and there are good connections with the hinterland. A clean and quieter port creates a kind of transitional zone with a nautical function instead of an urban one.

## PORT DEVELOPMENT

Urban development in proximity to port activities is no new phenomenon. A vision of urban development on the western banks of the IJ calls for a vision of the port development. Relocation is certainly not the only obvious strategy. By taking the continued presence of the port as a starting point, space is created for innovative solutions that may be a good deal more efficient in terms of costs, space and sustainability.

# 15. SILODAM, OUDE HOUTHAVEN AND HOUTHAVEN

The Oude Houthaven and Houthaven area that has been created along the elongated sea dyke to keep the water of the IJ out of the city was traditionally characterised by waterside industry: firms that depended on water for dispatch and supply, such as timber companies.

The western islands were already constructed around 1620 as part of the Third Extension of Amsterdam. Like the eastern islands, it was an area for activities related to shipping such as wharves, rope-making, sail-making, and tar and pitch storage.

The Oude Houthaven was created in its present form with the construction of the North Sea Canal in 1876. Warehouses like the Veem were in an optimal position here for transporting goods by water to and from the railway. Now the harbour is still in use by former skippers and commercial vessels.

The Houthaven was dug at the same time at the end of the nineteenth century as a result of the increasing activity in the area, which in turn led to the building of residential districts like the Zeeheldenbuurt and Spaarndammerbuurt. The inlet harbours were filled in after the war because timber was increasingly transported by road.

The dockland industry has gradually shifted westwards and for fifteen years the abandoned harbour terrain has been awaiting redevelopment. Because of the complex environmental aspects connected with a location next to the thriving harbour, the approval of plans at all levels (up to several hearings by the Council of State) has run up against many obstacles. Temporary functions such as housing for students and artists, a city beach and two school buildings bring life to the area.

The filled in harbours will be dug again, resulting in seven artificial islands for popular waterfront housing. According to the urban development plan of the district in cooperation with Sjoerd Soeters, it will become a low-traffic residential and business area with some 1,700 dwellings and 52,000 m2 of business space. The busy Spaarndammerdijk and the Tasmanstraat, which form the western connection between the centre and the A10 ring road, are expected to be led underground through tunnels to create a green area that will form a transition between the prewar residential districts and the new Houthaven.

## 15.1 WESTERDOKSHUIS

**Address:** Barentszplein 7
**Architect:** de architectengroep (Bjarne Mastenbroek)
**Client:** de architectengroep
**Year:** 1996

The area of the Barentszplein, the Zoutkeetsgracht and the Westerdoksdijk was wholly devoted to bread production in the nineteenth century. The Westerdokshuis was built in 1915 as a silo for flour transshipment; this building supplied the Amsterdam bakeries. De architectengroep later renovated the premises to install their own offices in a part of it. The solid wooden floors look like a patchwork cloak because at the time it was usual to transport flour vertically as much as possible, and to adjust the openings accordingly. Large voids on the sites of the silos create openness between the floors and allow daylight to reach the lower levels. The new entrance, robustly designed in wood and glass, is a striking feature in the façade.

## 15.2 CONCRETE GRAIN SILO

**Address:** Silodam 1-96
**Architect:** G. and J. D. Postma / Architectenbureau J. van Stigt
**Client:** De Principaal, Rabo Vastgoed
**Year:** 1952 / 1999

When the nineteenth-century stone grain silo was no longer adequate, a new one was built alongside it on the side facing the city in 1952 by the Postma brothers, who also did a lot of building work for the NDSM on the opposite bank. A large part of this building consisted of square silos (3.6 x 3.6 metres). They fell into disuse in the late 1980s and were soon afterwards squatted and used for accommodation and as work spaces. The silos were originally due for demolition so that tall tower blocks could be built on the site, but vigorous actions on the part of the squatters, locals and interested parties saved the silos from the wrecking ball. In 1990 they were declared protected historic buildings. The functionalist silo was transformed into a ten-storey block of flats with 89 apartments, most of them rented council property.
The apartments on the lowest floors still follow the dimensions of the grain silos. Larger rooms were obtained by breaking down the concrete walls between the shafts, which were sometimes as much as a metre thick.

## 15.3 STONE GRAIN SILO

**Address:** Silodam 100-256
**Architect:** Jacob F. Klinkhamer, A.L. van Gendt / Architectenbureau J. van Stigt
**Client:** J.Ph. Korthals Altes / Rabo Vastgoed
**Year:** 1896 / 2001

This brick silo was built in 1896 after a design by Klinkhamer and Van Gendt and commissioned by the trader and councillor Korthals Altes. The location on the west side of the city was unusual because, in spite of the opening of the North Sea Canal in 1876, most building activity had been confined to the eastern end of the docks. Korthals Altes, however, advocated the development of the western docks, as was to happen half a century later. Entirely in the spirit of its day, it was an industrial palace that expressed the importance of the grain trade at the time. The building had a classical composition with the storage space in the wings and weighing machinery, cleaning and office functions in the middle. The building became not only a local authority protected historic building but also a national one in the 1990s, which complicated its reuse as an apartment and business unit block. The apartment windows cut out of the stone façade mar the fortress-like appearance of the building, but they have been fitted naturally into the structure of the façade and the reinforced masonry support columns continue without interruption.

## 15.4 SILODAM

*A fully automatic car park has been installed underneath the Silodam on the basis of a slide puzzle system. You drive from the quay into the glass lift and leave your car in the lift shaft. When you press the button, your car is taken down to the compact underground car park with a capacity of 210 cars. There are always at least two lots free in that car park. When the car is summoned again, empty and loaded pallets are moved around until the right car reaches the lift.*

**Address:** Silodam 303-459
**Architect:** MVRDV
**Client:** De Principaal, Rabo Vastgoed
**Year:** 2002

Not just the volume, which has been conceived in this way for urban design reasons because of the relation to the two other existing silos, but the architecture and programme of this remarkable building too display a new dynamism in the field of housing that has been implemented on the riverbank, making it one of the major landmarks of the South Bank.
The complex consists of 142 owner-occupied apartments, 15 rented apartments in the social sector (including a 'commune' of senior citizens), business space, and underground parking in the pier. The apartments are divided into 'mini neighbourhoods' of four to eight similar typologies each, which are recognisable inside the building from the different colours of the corridors and access balconies. There are studios, workshops, maisonettes and lofts. The neighbourhoods can be recognised from the outside by the different materials and colours in the façade. The variegated composition of the façades refers to the big and colourful container ships that pass by every day.
A terrace has been built on the waterside that can be reached by non-residents as well by means of a broad wooden staircase. An anemometer on the roof automatically closes the windows of the terrace when the wind rises above force six to prevent the clientele from being swept away. To stop large vessels from entering, a dyke marked with buoys has been created underwater in the IJ.

## 15.5 IJSIDE

**Address:** Barentszplein 2-10
**Architect:** Tekton Architecten
**Client:** Eigen Haard, Rabo Vastgoed
**Year:** 2009

This housing and work complex with owner-occupied apartments, rented council apartments and business units forms a link between the Silodam and the Van Diemenstraat. The view of the docks from the street has been kept as open as possible because the building rests partly on piles. The entrances to the apartments are from the two inner courtyards. The business units on the street side at ground level include a dentist, a marketing and communications agency, and a firm of lawyers. The exterior is robust with concrete panels the colour of corten steel beneath a facet-like relief; the interior is finished with wood.

## 15.6 HET VEEM

**Address:** Van Diemenstraat 410-412
**Architect:** Roelof and Foeke Kuipers
**Client:** Het Nederlandsche Veem
**Year:** 1887

Het Veem warehouse was one of the first disused industrial buildings beside the IJ to be given a new function after having been squatted in the 1980s. The new users, who did up the premises on their own, have become trendsetters for the present informal and varied atmosphere beside the river.
Dating from the late nineteenth century, the Orange Nassauveem warehouse for the storage of luxury goods from the Dutch colonies such as coffee, tea, tobacco and cocoa, was given this name because it was built in the year of the coronation of Queen Wilhelmina. It was one of the first 'modern' warehouses on the west side of the harbour, with electrically driven cranes and lifts, flat, large floors supported by cast-iron columns, and a large load-bearing capacity. The brothers Roelof and Foeke Kuipers from the Dutch province of Friesland used predominantly Neo-Romanesque elements in the details of the yellow brick façades (arched windows, symmetrical composition) in the Van Diemenstraat, while the side facing the quay is in the more traditional idiom of the Amsterdam warehouse façade. Besides studios and workshops, there is a large exhibition space downstairs (de Veemvloer), while the room where consignments of tobacco used to be inspected, right at the top of the building, now houses a theatre. There is also a café-restaurant with a fantastic view of the IJ.

## 15.7 WESTERKEER SLUICE OPERATING POST

*One of the few physical reminders of the wood trade in the Nieuwe Houthaven is the waterside timber storage shed of Ambagtsheer Van der Meulen west of the approach to the Houthaven ferry, which used to be open to cars, but is now only for (motor) bikes and pedestrians.*

**Address:** Van Diemenstraat 422
**Architect:** ZICHT Architecten, ZILT Architecten
**Client:** Amsterdam Local Authority
**Year:** 2004

The design of the new operating post of the Westerkeer sluice had to comply with strict regulations, but these limiting conditions were also the starting point for the architects. The building had to be able to offer an unobstructed view, which is why the umbrella construction was chosen. This consists of a steel functional core which supports a roof that overhangs in all directions. This leaves the glass façade around the building clear of any obstruction. The light green colour, applied with a rubbery polyurethane coating, is an allusion to shipping, where this colour coating is used on steel decks. The walls of the conference room are printed with a seventeenth-century maritime scene to obtain the requisite sun protection.

## 15.8 PONTSTEIGER

**Address:** Tasmanstraat
**Architect:** Arons en Gelauff Architecten
**Client:** De Principaal, Bouwfonds MAB, Ymere, Rochdale
**Year:** 2015

A contemporary city gateway is planned at the tip of the ferry landing stage between the Silodam and the Houthaven area. The ambitious plan envisages a chair with a 90-metre back rest. Because the back rest is open and the building is raised seven metres above the pier, it conveys an airy appearance in spite of its size.
A catering establishment is planned 60 metres up with a panoramic view of the IJ, not to mention the fortunate residents of the 250 apartments with balconies.
In the future the ferries to North Amsterdam will depart from the east side of the building.

## 15.9 BONTE ZWAAN

**Address:** Haparandadam 7
**Architect:** NDSM / CASA architecten
**Client:** Vrachtmail / Woonstichting De Key
**Year:** 1966 / 2005

Although you would not say so at first sight, this floating 'breeding ground' with 22 studios, exhibition space and catering facilities already has a long past behind it. It was originally built in 1966 because of the shortage of space as the first floating office in the Netherlands for a subsidiary of the KNSM, with a mooring beside the Levantkade.
It employed a staff of 250 who had a pneumatic dispatch system at their disposal – the height of modernity at the time. The boat was used as a shipping fair in the 1980s. In 2003 it was transformed yet again into the present cultural 'breeding ground' under the name Bonte Zwaan [Speckled Swan].

## 15.10 QUBIC

**Address:** Stavangerweg 10-877, Gevleweg 20-91, 100-115
**Architect:** hvdn architecten
**Client:** De Principaal, Woonstichting De Key
**Year:** 2004

What was the site of firms related to the timber industry until recently is now a student campus, which can stay here until the construction of a new residential estate gets under way.
The hvdn firm of architects was given the unconventional assignment to design 715 student housing units in a very short space of time: there were twelve months between design and completion. Standard 3 x 9 metre residential containers (larger than the 2.5 x 5 metre containers used in shipping) were used with built-in prefab electric twin hot plates and a sink and toilet/shower unit. The blocks of stacked containers have white profiled prefab façade panels which are partly fitted with coloured Plexiglas.
An overhanging roof edge, supported by slender columns, forms a long veranda. The complex has a surrealist look about it and when seen from a distance it looks a bit like Le Corbusier's Nôtre-Dame du Haut in Ronchamp, the white sculptural church with the recessed horizontal stained glass windows from 1955.

## 15.11 HET 4E GYMNASIUM

**Address:** Stavangerweg 902
**Architect:** hvdn architecten
**Client:** Stadsdeel Westerpark Amsterdam, Esprit Scholen
**Year:** 2008

The relatively young 4e Gymnasium will be given a definitive location in the new Houthaven, but until then temporary accommodation has been implemented by the same firm of architects who designed the student accommodation next door.
The interim school building is modular to ensure optimal mobility so that it will be simple to use on other locations in Amsterdam afterwards. The classrooms and facilities are grouped around an enclosed yard.
The exterior is clad with wooden façade elements consisting of narrow, vertical battens set close together. The interior facing the yard where school life goes on is in bright orange.

## 15.12 STRAND WEST

**Address:** Stavangerweg 900
**Architect:** Total-X
**Client:** Strand West
**Year:** 2005

Like many others, Strand West [Beach West] was created as a temporary city beach. While Blijburg on IJburg moves on each year, this relaxed beach remains on the same spot – to the astonishment of the proprietors, who had expected to have to move on before now. But as long as it lasts, this beach pavilion – which lacks water for swimming – offers a prime location for a drink and a game of beach volleyball all year round.

## 15.13 PONT 13

**Address:** Haparandadam 50
**Architect:** Scheepsreparatie R. Langendijk
**Client:** R. Langendijk
**Year:** 1927 / 2005

The entrepreneur of the café-restaurant Pont 13 bought the ferryboat, which dates from 1927, for 'the price of scrap metal', after it had loyally served the municipal transport corporation for a long time crossing to and fro between the banks of the IJ, and had more recently been used to carry freight to IJburg. An authentic landing stage leads on board the industrial monument, which has been fitted out with an enormous wood stove, rough wooden ship's tables in the main area, and steel tables hanging from the side of the ship in the aisles, with old school chairs. The kitchen is predominantly French.

## 15.14 REM ISLAND

**Address:** Harparandadam
**Client:** Woonstichting De Key
**Year:** 1964 / 2011

Built as a prototype for a drilling platform, the steel construction was taken into use just outside the territorial waters in 1964 by the Reclame Exploitatie Maatschappij (REM). It broadcast the first commercial television in the Netherlands, including the US series *Mr. Ed the talking horse*. However, the anti-REM law put an end to the adventure after four months. Afterwards the platform was used as a measuring post by Public Works until 2006 and was then dismantled. De Key has taken over the platform minus the feet. An extra floor is being placed on top of the 22-metre construction painted red and white. The plans are for a restaurant on the top two floors with a panoramic terrace, and beneath it a social function related to the neighbourhood.

## 15.15 CULTURAL PODIUM

*A new connecting dam has been constructed between the Danzigerkade and the existing dyke for the development of the Houthaven. The dam is named after Haparanda, the easternmost point of Sweden on the border with Finland. This is the first landing stage for the Houthaven houseboat plan. Extra moorings for river craft have been implemented. A car park and a special car landing stage for loading or unloading a boat provide services for river skippers.*

**Address:** Harparandadam
**Architect:** NL Architects
**Client:** Haven Amsterdam with Roos Burger & Yvon IJzermans
**Year:** 2011

Two art historians were asked by the Port of Amsterdam to give the Houthaven a cultural boost. The cultural podium at the end of the Harparandadam is a part of the programme. The design competition was won by NL Architects. Multi Mill consists of three different wings connected by a central platform. Each of them can serve a different purpose: catwalk, cinema, stage. Moreover, the mill can rotate so that a different background forms the décor for each event.

McG

# 16. MINERVAHAVEN, MERCURIUSHAVEN, VLOTHAVEN AND COENHAVEN

The Damrak, where the River Amstel runs into the IJ north of Dam Square, was already in use as a harbour in the early Middle Ages and continued in that function down to the sixteenth century, followed by extensions eastwards and westwards in the succeeding centuries.
The character of the Amsterdam harbour has changed drastically. The harbour is now an international logistical centre where the large-scale storage and transshipment of commodities proceeds in parallel with their industrial processing. The largest part of the Westpoort, the zone of the city including the harbour and that is administered by Amsterdam Harbour, thus lies outside the A10 ring road and extends along the bank of the IJ via the North Sea Canal to IJmuiden. While in the past the harbour was inextricably a part of the life of the city and its residents, the dockside activities now take place almost entirely out of sight of all those who do not work in the harbour. That is why people often forget that Amsterdam has the fourth largest harbour in Europe. However, a small part of the active harbour area is situated within the A10 ring road around the Minervahaven, the Mercuriushaven, the Vlothaven and the Coenhaven.
The Minervahaven and the Nieuwe Houthaven, which used to be the location for timber transshipment and related production, storage, building and transport companies that had moved from the centre, are gradually being incorporated in the fabric of the city. A development vision under the name Minerva City Harbour has been drawn up based on the principle that the zone must gradually and organically be transformed into an urban business location for the creative industry such as advertising agencies and firms of architects. Small-scale nautical firms are still welcome. In the present situation most of the businesses have turned their back on the water because of the transshipment function that is still operative. But it is the waterfront that has a future, with a quay that is as open to the public as possible. The Minervahaven cannot be used for housing as long as the industrial activities with specific environmental restrictions continue to exist west of the Mercuriushaven. All the same, the Minervahaven is a buffer zone for the housing in the Houthaven.
Larger transshipment and food processing companies are grouped around the Mercuriushaven, the Vlothaven and the Coenhaven. Commodities are transported by rail, road and water. The Second Coentunnel is under construction to relieve the A10 West ring road. The environment on land is not designed for a cycle ride or a stroll, but it is certainly impressive.

## 16.1 BUSINESS COMPLEX

**Address:** Danzigerkade 17
**Architect:** Dedato ontwerpers en architecten
**Client:** Danzigerkade Beheer
**Year:** 2002

This business complex for small-scale creative enterprises, where Dedato itself was initially accommodated, is the first new building of the quality that is being aimed at in the planning zone. The modern no-nonsense style won the firm several other commissions in the Minervahaven. The 50-metre deep complex with a front and a rear building looks fresh and businesslike, but above all uncomplicated, with its simple prefab concrete structure and large casement doors with terraces. The design is based on the idea that every part of the interior must offer a view of the IJ and the Minervahaven. This has been achieved by means of the transparent front and rear façades and by keeping the area below the high ceiling on each floor open.

## 16.2 BARTS HEAD OFFICE

**Address:** Danzigerkade 11
**Architect:** Dedato ontwerpers en architecten
**Client:** Nemaco
**Year:** 2006

What was once started up by a boy selling shorts on the beaches of Saint-Tropez has grown to become a leading European retailer of woollen hats, scarves and other accessories with its head office in the Minervahaven, designed by the house architects of the zone. Given its function as a distribution centre, it has a closed ground floor, with large concrete entrances on the quay for the goods transport. A striking wooden door is the main entrance. Daylight enters via a continuous strip of windows and glass building bricks. The second floor, where the design studios are situated, has a wooden façade inspired by the rough beams that used to be unloaded and processed in the Houthavens.

## 16.3 COASTERS AND BARGES FOR LIVING AND WORKING

**Address:** Minervahavenweg

There are a number of moorings for freight vessels without a motor beside the Minervahavenweg. These vessels are used as flexible storage depots for the IGMA company, a subsidiary of Cargill, that takes care of the transshipment of bulk cargoes varying from agricultural products to coal and minerals. Every now and then the boats cross to the other side to be loaded or unloaded, after which they return to their moorings. The skippers live on them. Enormous coasters regularly moor on the north side of the quay, where there is a place for ships from all over the world to pass the time between arriving on the IJ and loading and/or unloading dry bulk. When one of these ships arrives in the Minervahaven, a message is passed on to De Koperen Ploeg, a cooperative of steersmen and other dockhands who help the ocean-going vessels to moor and drop anchor safely by casting and hauling up the hawsers.

## 16.4 DANZIGER BOCHT

**Address:** Danzigerbocht 35
**Client:** Bureau Broedplaats Gemeente Amsterdam
**Year:** 2002

*Many businesses dependent on water have settled on the Danzigerkade, such as a company that repairs the sides of the canals. This is also the location of the depository of the Department of Inland Water Management, the 'detention centre' for all confiscated vessels. The longitudinal embankment has a harbour for flat-bottom craft.*

The Amsterdam local authority's 'cultural breeding ground' policy is an indirect consequence of the development of the banks of the IJ, where many refuges for artists arose in old (squatted) premises over the years. When these were increasingly cleared out to make room for new projects, the artists united and, in cooperation with the artists' union (FNV), submitted a request to the city council for 'a constructive settlement policy for this target group of young cultural economic growth', in other words, for new studios. In 2000 the local authority voted to earmark funds for this purpose and even to set up a separate project group for it. By 2004 more than 539 places had been found on 24 locations, many of them on the banks of the IJ. This policy enabled the TransformArt group of artists to find a collective studio in this warehouse, which is inconspicuously located at the back of a sawmill. It accommodates five temporary studios.

## 16.5 YDEK

**Address:** Archangelkade 8
**Architect:** Dedato ontwerpers en architecten
**Client:** G&S Vastgoed / Rick Engelkes Producties
**Year:** 2011

The renewal that is already under way on the Danzigerkade is gradually spreading to the west: the area around the Minervahaven. This inlet is the heart of the old Houthavens, now known as Minerva City Harbour. Ydek is a multifunctional office and business complex made of concrete, glass, wood and aluminium to provide flexible workfloors for the creative industry with parking on the premises. Rick Engelkes Productions, which operates in television and other multimedia, is the main user. Various sustainable interventions have been made in the building, such as heat or cold retention via the ground water, concrete core activation, and green roofing where possible.

## 16.6 KPN-DIGITENNE TRANSMISSION MAST

There is a 115-metre transmission mast with an antenna for digital television on the Nieuwe Hemweg. It provides coverage for a large part of Zaanstad and Amsterdam; together with the station on the South Axis, it caters for the entire city. It is illuminated at night by a work of art in lights designed by the light architect Har Hollands, whose work can be seen in many unusual projects all over the world, including the Egyptian pyramids in Gizeh and the Rembrandt Tower in Amsterdam. He transformed the mast into a beacon for the city with the colours red and white, thereby referring both to a lighthouse and to the harbour and the civic colours of Amsterdam. The lighting consists of LED armatures with a programmable central operating system that can regulate the intensity of each LED light. As a result, the appearance of the mast is constantly changing at night. If you pass it in the evening you may see a white mast with red pulsating light on the antenna, while on the way back it may look like a lighthouse with its typical red and white markings.

**Address:** Nieuwe Hemweg
**Artist:** Har Hollands
**Year:** 2010

## 16.7 VAN GANSEWINKEL SPIT

**Address:** Nieuwe Hemweg 8

'Refuse does not exist' is the motto of the Van Gansewinkel refuse treatment company situated at the end of the spit between the Vlothaven and the Neptunushaven. The company collects waste from businesses and sorts it for reuse. Many of the activities are not accessible to the public and can only be watched from a distance. The Amsterdam and Neptune warehouses on the quay store jute sacks filled with cocoa beans.

## 16.8 CARGILL B.V.

**Address:** Coenhavenweg 2
**Year:** 1959

The originally US Cargill food concern, which started in the Netherlands in 1959 as a commodity retail organisation, has grown to become one of the largest European enterprises in the field of the production of food ingredients and the processing, marketing and distribution of agricultural products. The firm has 2,300 employees on various locations in the Netherlands. It is mainly grains and oil seeds that are processed in Amsterdam, such as soya beans, sunflower seed and coleseed, which accounts for the strange smell that sometimes pervades the surroundings. Cargill has opposed the local authority's plans for the urban development of the Houthaven since the 1990s. The food concern and the harbour firms nearby are afraid that the advent of housing on their doorstep will lead to a tightening of environmental regulations. After a long legal battle, an agreement was reached in 2008. The planned housing will go ahead, but the local authority has promised not to come up with new building plans in the next fifteen years. Moreover, the local authority will release funds so that the companies can satisfy the new environmental regulations.

## 16.9 DE PARLEVINKER

**Address:** Coenhavenweg 28
**Year:** 1902

Since the beginning of the last century, De Parlevinker used to visit the vessels in the harbours to sell its wares, but now that every freight vessel has a car on board, the travelling sales boat is permanently moored in the Coenhaven. Today it is the harbour workmen who visit the floating shop for breakfast and lunch, as well as to buy boots, overalls and other practical items.

## 16.10 COENTUNNEL

**Client:** Rijkswaterstaat
**Year:** 1966 / 2012

The Coentunnel links the Zaanstreek with the west of Amsterdam. The tunnel of almost 1.5 kilometres in length is named after the neighbouring Coenhaven, which in turn is named after the colonist Jan Pieterszoon Coen. The tunnel was called for because the Hempont could no longer handle the increasing traffic. Cars sometimes had to wait three quarters of an hour before they could cross to the other side of the North Sea Canal. The double two-lane tunnel, constructed in a temporary dock on the other side that was created specially for it in what is now the Cornelis Douwes terrain, was officially opened by Queen Juliana in 1966. In its first decades the tunnel was a great success, but with the increase in traffic it is now mainly filled with traffic jams as part of the A10 West ring road. The Second Coentunnel will improve the flow of traffic.

ELM

over
hoeks

# PUBLIC TRANSPORT

## FERRY SERVICES

There are five ferries between the two banks of the IJ. Except for IJ ferry XIII, they are all free of charge and service pedestrians, cyclists and mopeds.

**Houthaven ferry**
The Houthaven ferry operates between the Tasmanstraat in the Oude Houthaven and the NDSM wharf. It runs three times an hour on working days from 06:45 to 24:00 hours, twice an hour between 10:00 and 16:00 hours, and four times an hour in the weekend from 09:00 to 24:00 hours. The crossing takes about six minutes.

**Distelweg ferry**
The Distelweg ferry operates between the Tasmanstraat in the Oude Houthaven and the Distelweg at the westernmost point of Buiksloter-ham. It only runs on working days, twice an hour from 06:30 to 19:30 hours, with three or four crossings per hour in the peak period. The crossing takes about seven minutes.
For a long time it was also possible to take cars on the Distelweg ferry because the crossing formed part of the route for transporting danger-ous substances, but since 2007 that route has been diverted via the Schellingwouderbrug or via the Hempont between the Hemhavens and Zaandam.

**NDSM wharf ferry**
The NDSM wharf ferry operates between the Central Station and the NDSM terrain. It operates on working days twice an hour between 07:00 and 01:00 hours, and four times an hour during the peak period. In the weekend it operates twice an hour between 9:00 and 24:00 hours, and until 01:00 hours on Saturday. The crossing takes about fourteen minutes.

**Buiksloterweg ferry**
The Buiksloterweg ferry operates between the Central Station and the Buiksloterweg. The ferry operates 24 hours a day. It leaves every six minutes, or every twelve minutes at night and at some hours during the weekend. The crossing takes about five minutes.

**IJplein ferry**
The IJplein ferry operates between the Central Station and the Pontplein (formerly the IJplein). It operates between 6:00 and 24:00 hours from Monday to Saturday and between 9:00 and 24:00 hours on Sunday.
It leaves four times an hour, and five to eight times an hour during the peak period. The crossing takes about five minutes.

**IJ ferry XIII**
The IJ ferry XIII is one of the small IJ ferries that carried passengers only until 1971. It has been kept as a museum ferry. It leaves three times every Sunday from May to October from landing stage 14 behind the Central Station for a two-hour round trip past the following stops: Azartplein (KNSM island), Levantplein (KNSM island), Sporenburg, and Nieuwendammerdijk (Cafe 't Sluisje).

## BUS SERVICES

**South**
Line 22: Indische Buurt – Spaarndammerbuurt (via Prins Hendrikkade)
Line 48: Sloterdijk Station – Central Station (via Westerdok and Houthavens)
Line 42: KNSM island – Central Station
Line 43: Borneo island – Central Station
Line 237: Sloterdijk Station – Coenhaven
Line 238: Sloterdijk Station – Hempontplein

**North**
Line 30: Holysloot – Buikslotermeerplein (via Schellingwoude)
Line 32: Buikslotermeerplein – Central Station (via Vogelbuurt)
Line 38: Molenwijk – Nieuwendam Amerbos (via Buiksloterham and the Hamerstraat district)
Line 91: Central Station – Zaandam (via Cornelis Douwes terrain)
Line 94: Central Station – Zaandam NS (via Cornelis Douwes terrain)

## TRAM SERVICES

**South**
Line 25: Pres. Kennedylaan – PTA Station (via Central Station)
Line 26: Central Station – IJburg (via Piet Heinkade)

# ABOUT THE AUTHORS

**Pito Dingemanse** studied social geography and later worked for the National Physical Planning Agency and the Council for Infrastructure and the Environment. Since 2003 he has been head of Planning and Environment for Port of Amsterdam, where he is responsible for the spatial development of the harbour. For the last few years he has been head of the Haven-Stad long-term research project.

**Ronald Hooft** trained as an artist and designer. Since 2002 he has been a partner in PrastHooft Architects, a firm in Amsterdam that designs interiors for catering establishments, hotels, offices, shops and private homes. He presented the architecture feature in the TV programme *KunstUur* and has a weekly column on a building in Amsterdam in *Het Parool*.

**Maarten Kloos** is co-founder and director of ARCAM (Architecture Centre Amsterdam), where he has organised many debates and exhibitions on developments in the Amsterdam region. He has taught in various institutions, including the Technical University Delft and the Amsterdam Academy of Architecture, and has written many articles in Dutch and foreign periodicals, such as *wonen-TA/BK*, *Archis*, *L'Architecture d'Aujourd'hui*, *Werk* and *Bauen + Wohnen*. He is co-editor of the series *Amsterdam Architecture* (ARCAM Pocket), and the (co-)author of books including *In a manner of seeing* (2000), *Formats for living: Contemporary floor-plans in Amsterdam* (2000), *25 buildings you should have seen* (2002), *Mooring site Amsterdam* (2007) and *Searching for space: On the architect Herman Hertzberger* (2010).

**Sabine Lebesque** is an architecture historian and consultant for the Amsterdam Development Corporation (OGA). This function has involved her in the *Projectenboek*, the Zuiderkerk Award for the best architect and principal of the year, the series *Stappen door de nieuwe stad, tochten langs de jongste woningbouw* (2001), excursions abroad, the building inspectorate, and the TV programme *Aanbouw* (AT5). From 1991 to 2000 she worked for the Netherlands Architecture Institute in Rotterdam, where she was responsible for various projects, including the exhibition and publication *Yona Friedman, structures serving the unpredictable* (1998). In 2007 she wrote the Valiz publication *Along Amsterdam's Waterfront, Exploring the architecture of Amsterdam's Southern IJ Bank* on behalf of the OGA and the ProjectmanagementBureau Amsterdam, published by Valiz.

**Harkolien Meinsma** studied social geography and planning before setting up Bureau Meinsma redactionele producties, which organises productions and publications on densification, land policy and building regulations. It has also organised exhibitions such as 'Female architects in Amsterdam' and 'Always on the move', about the work of architects from the former Dutch colonies. In 2000 she wrote the advisory report 'The green bank of the IJ, the riverside of North Amsterdam outside the dyke', which is now the blueprint for the transformation of the North Bank of the IJ. She is currently coordinating Light on the IJ, a group of five light artists who are developing and exhibiting inspiring visual ideas for the IJ in 2011.

**Ton Schaap** graduated from the Architecture Academy Amsterdam in 1983. He is an urban planner and works for the Amsterdam local authority. He has been working since 1987 on the banks of the IJ from the Houthavens to IJburg.

# INDEX OF PERSONS AND ARCHITECTS

# INDEX OF STREET NAMES

# PROJECTS INDEX

# ACKNOWLEDGE-MENTS

**With thanks to all the architects and principals who provided information and illustrative material.**

**With grateful acknowledgements to:**
Kees and Bonnie Alberts (Historical Centre North), Matthijs Kok (Noordwaarts and South IJ Bank project bureau), Sjanet Wagemanns (Communications, Noordwaarts Planning Office), Harkolien Meinsma (ANGSAW), René Grotendorst (former director Noordwaarts Planning Office), Ronald Janssen.

**This publication was made possible thanks to the generous contribution of the following organisations and persons:**

- L'Abattoir
- St. AIM
- AM Wonen
- Amstel Botel
- Amvest
- Architecten Bureau Dijkstra
- de Architekten Cie.
- Ch. Brinkhuis
- B. Bulten
- F. van den Burght
- CZAN
- S. Dielemans
- DMO
- S. van den Eickhof
- G & S Vastgoed
- H. Gerson
- Hilton Amsterdam
- J.P.C. Hofstee
- IBA
- E. Jepma
- C. de Jong
- St. Kennisoever
- P. Klomp
- Lamarque
- J. van Leeningen
- W. van Leuven
- MAB
- Nauta Dutilh
- Omniplan
- Piet Hein Buildings
- Projectbureau Noordwaarts
- Projectbureau Wibaut aan de Amstel
- Projectbureau Zuidoostlob
- S. Rhebergen
- Rijnboutt Architecten
- E.J.J. de Rooij
- G. Ruijsink
- J. Schuil
- SD+P
- Slavenburg
- S. Soeters
- SPINN
- Stadgenoot
- Stadia
- D. Stadig
- Stadsarchief
- A.M. Teppema
- Vast Janszen
- H. van Veldhuizen
- J. Visser
- Vos & Vos-Panhuijsen
- S. Wagemanns
- M. Zonnevylle

Gemeente Amsterdam
Noordwaarts

Gemeente Amsterdam
Stadsdeel Noord

Gemeente Amsterdam
Ontwikkelingsbedrijf

Gemeente Amsterdam
ProjectManagement Bureau

Gemeente Amsterdam
Projectbureau Zuidelijke IJoever

ASR vastgoed

Vastgoedontwikkeling
BOELENS de GRUYTER
Vastgoedbeleggingen

BIESTERBOS
making worlds

ING
Real Estate Development

vesteda

Ymere
wonen, leven, groeien

IJDock

EIGEN HAARD gewoon goed in wonen

# COLOPHON

The information in this guide has been compiled from a large variety of sources of information: internet, websites of all kinds, various books, reports, policy documents, newspaper articles, interviews with the civil servants involved, users, passers-by and above all personal observation. Of course the aim has been to present the facts as correctly as possible. If you come across any incorrect information, we ask you to report it to *s.lebesque@oga.amsterdam.nl* so that it can be taken into account in any future publications.
Some of the projects were already covered in *Along Amsterdam's Waterfront. Exploring the architecture of Amsterdam's Southern IJ Bank* (ISBN 13-978-90-78088-12-7). That guide was confined to the southern bank of the IJ, but went further inland and did not extend beyond the eastern and western islands.

The illustrations marked with an asterisk * are artist's impressions, drawings or photographs of models of projects that are (not yet) under construction.

Most of the people portrayed in this guide are aware that their image might be used for this publication. If you recognise yourself, you can contact the publisher to receive a copy of the publication.

Compilation and author: Sabine Lebesque, Amsterdam Development Corporation (OGA), commissioned by Noordwaarts Planning Office, Amsterdam
Assistant: Caroline Uittenbroek
Photography: Sabine Lebesque
Photography projects 12.16, 12.17, 15.12, 16.4: Johan Olsthoorn
Authors theme texts: Pito Dingemanse, Ronald Hooft, Maarten Kloos, Harkolien Meinsma, Ton Schaap
Translation: Peter Mason
Copy editing: Els Brinkman
Cartography: Dienst Persoons- en Geo-informatie, Gemeente Amsterdam, adapted by De Designpolitie, thanks to Alfons Wezenberg
Graphic design: De Designpolitie, Amsterdam
Production: Astrid Vorstermans
Lithography and printing: Die Keure, Bruges (B)
Publisher: Valiz, Amsterdam



valiz

Available in the Netherlands, Belgium and Luxemburg via Centraal Boekhuis, Culemborg; Scholtens, Sittard; and Coen Sligting Bookimport, Alkmaar, NL, sligting@xs4all.nl, fax +31-(0)72-5117029
Available in Europe (except Benelux, UK and Ireland), Asia and Australia through Idea Books, Amsterdam, NL, idea@ideabooks.nl, fax +31-20-6209299
Available in the United Kingdom and Ireland through Art Data, London, UK, orders@artdata.co.uk, fax +44-208-742 2319
Available in North, South and Central America through D.A.P./ Distributed Art Publishers Inc, www.artbooks.com, fax + 212 6279484
All other questions: please contact Valiz, info@valiz.nl

www.valiz.nl

www.noordwaarts.nl

*Around Amsterdam's IJ Banks*
ISBN: 978-90-78088-48-6

Also available in Dutch: *Het IJ Rondom*
ISBN: 978-90-78088-47-9

NUR 648

Printed and bound in Belgium